TWO HEARTS COLLIDE

Written by Connie Miller

COPYRIGHT 2014 Connie Miller

All Rights Reserved

ISBN-13: 9780692385128

Dedication

I want to dedicate this book to my wonderful husband, Willie Miller. If it were not for your commitment to allow God to love me through you, I would not have risen up to be all that God purposed for me to be. I am so proud to call you my husband. Working side by side with you in ministry is one of the greatest privileges God has given me. The anointing that we have, as a couple, is powerful, exciting, and growing as we both walk together with the Lord. I look forward to each day and seeing how He will use us. Thank you for loving me just as I was, just as I am, and just as I will be as God transforms me more. I love you so very much!

Your Wiffy,
Connie

Acknowledgements

I would like to give honor and thanks to my adopted mom, Donna, and my late father, Leo Dorsey. God chose you to be my adopted parents and I am so glad He did. You gave me unconditional love and a home that was stable and secure. I love you both so very much. You are and always will be my parents!

I want to say a big, "I LOVE YOU," to my three children; Holly, Kendra, and Trevor. You are awesome and God has big plans for each of you. As you read this book, I pray God will speak to your hearts in very personal ways. Thank you for your unconditional love.

Forward

My wife, Connie, was born in March, 1969 in less than ideal circumstances. Her mother was just barely 16 when she arrived. About a year after Connie's birth, Connie's grandmother passed away leaving Connie's mother devastated. In the midst of all her mother's pain and turmoil, Connie's mother made the very difficult decision to put her nearly two-year-old daughter up for adoption. Although this was the absolute best decision Connie's mother could have made for her daughter, this was just the beginning of Satan whispering lies, producing deep-seated roots of rejection and abandonment in Connie's life.

Connie was adopted. But, after six months and for reasons unknown, she was returned to the adoption agency. Connie was then adopted into a permanent, loving family, but battled with insecurity. She was often made fun of by her peers as the "chubby girl". The teasing reinforced her feelings of being rejected and the roots grew deeper. In trying to be accepted, she began to be promiscuous at a very young age. Each young man that would show sexual interest towards her would give her the feeling of being pretty and that she was accepted. While in high school, Connie became involved in a serious relationship. The relationship became abusive and ended when Connie became pregnant. Connie was now the single, teenage parent.

Connie would find the years ahead to be filled with addiction, emotional instability, and a very unhealthy marriage. The emotional pain of her first marriage was magnified by her husband's infidelities. She divorced him, but she remarried him a few years later with the hope that since she now knew Jesus things would be different. It was not. It would only be a few years before she found herself divorcing him a second time. In her devastation and brokenness, Connie cried out to God. She asked God to bring her a man that loved Him first and who wanted to serve Him. She desperately wanted, and needed, a healthy, God-centered relationship. She decided to wait on God and allow Him to bring her the man that He wanted for her. It was almost two years later that God answered her prayer and Connie and I met.

When I think of how I would describe Connie, it is difficult. If I were to say beautiful, smart, kind or compassionate, it would only describe a portion of her such as her character or looks. To truly describe her, the best example is a rose seed. A seed, in its beginning, is not really much to look at, but the potential, for it becoming beautiful, is great! If a person takes a rose seed and plants it in the ground, waters it and nurtures it, a sprout will soon emerge. Not long after the sprout makes its way through the crust of the earth, it begins to grow a leaf, then another, and another, and so-on. Soon that stem produces small buds on the end of each branch. Then, on a warm spring morning, the bud blooms and becomes a beautiful flower; a rose. This describes Connie. This book is her journey of becoming a rose. The only thing is Connie did not see herself as a rose seed in the beginning, but God did! On the day I met her, God allowed me to see the rose still in the form of a seed waiting to be watered and nurtured. God has brought forth the rose! This book is the emotional journey of God transforming her from a seed into that beautiful rose.

Written by William Miller

Introduction

The empty pages of a fresh new journal bring me such excitement. They are not just ordinary pages, but pages that become filled with everything that is hidden within my heart.

As I write to my wonderful Lord, I begin to sense a vibrant, exciting relationship developing with Him. He has made me a true writer at heart. Writing is a gift that He put in me while I was being formed in my mother's womb. He patiently waited until the time was right for this precious gift to be manifested in my life. You see, it is where my pen meets the page that my heart and God's heart collide. On these pages, I am free to give Him all that is in my heart. There are some days that I feel my heart is very far from Him but, that is ok because He accepts me right where I am. As I write in my honesty, He has a way of trading all the bad and imparting into me all that He is. As I fill the pages, I begin to see clearly His heart towards me. I am able to see the endless possibilities in my life as I walk with Him. As I seek Him more on the empty pages of my journal, I have a growing trust that He will write His thoughts to me through my own hand.

For many years, I struggled to hear God's voice and know clearly what He was saying to me. I would try to pray in my head, but this was very difficult for me. Then one day, when I was at the end of myself, dealing with a failing marriage, I sat down and started journaling. *Empty Without You* was the first writing that was given to me in that moment. It felt good to see my feelings on paper. I had no idea, at the time, what was being birthed in my life. I just knew I had to get out of my own head so that I could have clarity instead of confusion. I began journaling almost daily. It felt good to write my feelings to the Lord. I began to think, 'It's not enough for me to always be expressing myself to God. I need to hear Him and what He is saying to me.' So, I began writing what would come to my mind as if it were God. At first, I was wary and unsure of how much of it was me, what I wanted God to say, and how much was really Him. As I would write, I would often feel that it was me and what I wanted to hear. Then, as I would read it back to myself, it would melt my heart. It didn't feel like me. It didn't take me long to see how He was just waiting for me to realize that He so very much wanted to have a two-way conversation with me on the empty pages.

The passion grew in me for writing. I had a new anticipation that the empty pages would be filled with words from my Daddy God's heart that were meant for me.

The more I wrote these cherished words from my Daddy God, the more He impressed upon me that there are many others who need to know His true heart for them. So many people, myself included, have had a wrong perception of who God is and how He sees us.

Although I had cried out to Jesus in my early 20's to save me, there was so much that I did not understand about His grace. I had grown up in church and was taught religion. I had no clue how to have a personal relationship with God. My perception was that as long as I did well, or what I thought was good, God was pleased with me. When I didn't, I felt He was mad at me. This wrong perception of God created a constant insecurity in His love. I found myself in a cycle of pulling away from God, and embracing sinful ways, only to return to Him later emotionally exhausted. I was plagued with continual condemnation and a fear of God that resulted in emotional torment. Can anyone relate to this? I am sure there are many who do, but may never admit it.

Although I was a Christian, I had two failed marriages to the same man. I had many addictions, anger problems, insecurity, and abandonment issues. I could not see how God could love me and accept me since I kept messing up. How could I call myself a Christian? Am I even really saved? What if it wasn't for real? These were some of the thoughts that would plague me. Darkness would often engulf me.

Then, on Nov 3, 2009, my whole life changed. God in His

wisdom knew what I needed and what it would take for me to really begin to understand His love and grace. God had heard my cry when I asked Him to send to me a Christian man; a man who truly loved Him and wanted to serve Him. He sent me a one-legged Pastor named Willie Miller.

God was promoting me to a position of influence as a Pastor's wife; even while I was in the midst of a pain pill addiction. Now, that is grace! I had received unmerited, undeserved favor from God Almighty. As my husband allowed God to love me through him, I began to see what God's love was really like. This man was like no other I had met. I felt safe and that I could finally trust someone with my brokenness. I was able to be honest and not hide in myself. Willie loved me as I went through the process of letting go of the pills. Willie loved me through my periods of anger when I had no clue why I was angry. He showed me compassion. I was literally being loved with the hands, arms, and feet of God through this man.

As I began to study the Bible more diligently, God gave me a new understanding of His Word. I began teaching God's Word and, at the same time as I was teaching God's Word, God was teaching me. I was learning how to really love people. God was breaking the chains. He was helping me to see that it was never about what I had done, but what had been done for me by His Son, Jesus. I wasn't standing in my own works, but the finished work of Jesus Christ. I was made right because of Jesus. There was nothing I could do to change that. I started to feel some security in His love for me. The strongholds of rejection and insecurity began to be broken.

Now, through the Lord's leading, I am sharing a glimpse of my journey with its many ups and downs; and, the relationship with God that has developed through the years. My prayer is that as you read this, your heart will also collide with God's heart. God has chosen to love you passionately with an everlasting love. When you are at your worst, God chooses to stay with you. God has you covered by the blood of His Son, Jesus-all the way into eternity!

GOD'S HEART~

TRAVEL WITH ME

My Dear Child,

Lose yourself in Me. Get lost in My perfect love. There you will find all you need. No more dead-end roads, but endless highways that will take you where you never have imagined. I will say, 'Turn here,' and you will easily follow. Because once you have experienced My perfect love, you will trust that the way I have for you is best. Our journey together will be exciting and passionate. There will be times I will take you to the mountain top. There you will see new and glorious things. I will use you in mighty ways to show My glory to others.
Here is where you will know that you can do anything because I am with you. You will see the purpose I have for you.
Then, there will be times when we will travel through the valleys of the unknown. There will be many twists and turns. The enemy will try to take you back down the dead-end road. Notice I said, 'We will travel these valleys.' I won't leave you. I will be with you; lighting the road and teaching you as you go. You will learn how to hear and see Me. In these valleys I will be helping you unpack the suitcases that you don't need. In these suitcases, we will find many things. Things such as fear, pride, envy, addictions, distrust, and the list continues. You will try to hang onto some of these things; but, as we travel this valley, you will learn the road will be easier to travel without them. As you throw those old suitcases away, one-by-one, your load will be lighter and we will be able to get to the mountain top faster. Soon, you will wonder why you needed those old suitcases, anyway. This is what getting lost in My love will do. Getting lost in My love is when you will see that you have been found. You will have clear direction. You are on the road to your destination. Eternity with Me!

Your Daddy,
God

1 John 5:13(NLT) "I have written this to you who believe in the name of the Son of God, so that you may know you have eternal life.

MY HEART~

Journal Entry 9-4-03

It's easier to be angry, to push people away, than to feel the pain of being let down, abandoned, and betrayed. All my life, I've pushed people away with my anger. Maybe, I pushed people away because I feared they would leave me. Maybe, I pushed people away so I could feel I had control of my life. It is very hard to love completely and be vulnerable. Sooner or later, we all have to leave the ones we love. I hate it! I think with that fact, and the fact that I was adopted out at age 2, I have a very hard time trusting anyone. Who can be trusted? Even the ones who are supposed to love me the most, end up hurting me. If I don't leave them first, they will just leave me. I guess that's why I have a very hard time believing that You are not going to leave me Lord, no matter how bad I've been. It's so hard for me to trust You with all of my life. I want the control, Lord, but the more I try to have control, the less I really have. I wish I could just lay it all down but at this point I just can't, Lord. I need You to teach me how to trust You, to let this pain go. It's eating me up inside. I am hurting others because of my very own hurt. Forgive me. It seems when I'm feeling my worst about myself is when I point out other people's faults. Why is that? Is it so I don't have to think of myself?

EMPTY WITHOUT YOU

Everywhere I turn the temptations call my name; promising me things that I will gain, pleasure I can obtain.

I've been down this road a hundred times, chasing, seeking all the vain imaginations of my mind.

EMPTY, EMPTY, EMPTY, that's what I feel. Even with Your promises that I know are real. Here You are waiting to fill me up and yet I run to that other stuff.

Will I ever get it? Will I ever change? When will You be just enough?

I get so tired and confused. This should be easy and obvious. I've learned Your lessons so many times. Yet, each time is like the first time, learning it over and over, like a little child who forgets.

One day, I pray You'll be enough. Then, I can get rid of this awful junk. But, until I do, EMPTY is what I will be without YOU!

GOD'S HEART~

TRUST ME

My Dear Child,

Trusting Me, that is the root of your problem. You cannot fix things or find a solution to all the things that burden you. I know your burdens. You are not meant to carry them. Let Me do it. Just listen for My voice and follow. That's all you need to do. You are making it hard to hear My voice. I am always speaking, desiring for you to hear Me. Listen and draw near. Get quiet before Me! Seek My Word! It is My very voice.

Nothing you are chasing will satisfy or be the answer. Chase after Me! Only, I won't run. I will be where I've always been; in front of you, behind you, and beside you. Think on Me continually. Train yourself, your mind, and I will take care of you and everything else for it belongs to Me. Trust and rest My Child!

Your Daddy,
God

Psalm 62:89(NASV) "Trust in him at all times, O people; pour out your heart before him; God is a refuge for us."

MY HEART~

Journal Entry 9-10-03

I thank You, Lord, for a good day. Lord, You have blessed my life with a wonderful job that I did not deserve. Help me to graciously submit to the authorities above me. I confess to You that I do not do this well. It was wonderful starting out my day with worship music. It makes all the difference. I need a whole new mindset, Lord. Give me Your thoughts. I need to forsake my sin of gluttony. I ask to once and for all be totally changed in this area. I'm tired of running to food.

Journal Entry 11-12-03

Here, I sit in the darkest places of my soul. I am such an evil, horrible person at times. The heart truly is deceitful. I have so many problems. I'm so discouraged at having gained my weight back. I worked so hard to lose it and here I am again. I feel like a failure. I'm tired! I am a food addict. I turn to it for everything. Will I ever change? I see how my children have the same problem. I also have a problem with depression.

YET THERE YOU ARE

How evil we are at the deepest part of ourselves. Yet, there You are.

The lies we tell ourselves and the things we chase after. Yet, there You are.

So much hurt we put each other through with words that cut like knives. Yet, there You are. We wake up every day, going about our lives as if it is ours. Thinking we are in control. Yet, still, You are there; Loving us, waiting for us, tending to our needs when we don't even realize it.

You have always been there, our ever-faithful Creator. Oh, if we would just see the love and tenderness You lavish on us.

We need to open our eyes and look to the cross. Then, we will see just how much it cost to show us You'd always be there for us.

Journal Entry 2-14-04

Here I am, Lord. It's been so long since I've written and talked to You. How ashamed I am of myself that I call myself a Christian and yet, hardly, even talk to You. Forgive me, Lord. I miss You, I do. It's just the world gets in my way. I get so distracted. Lord, why do I fear dying and seeing You if love is supposed to cast out all fear? I ask, once again, for peace in the moments before my death. I don't want to be afraid. I want to be excited to meet You face-to-face. Please accept me, Jesus, into Your Kingdom. I realize and believe You are the only way.

Lord, reveal to me what it truly means to be free in You. What measure of faith is enough to be saved? There's so much that I don't understand. We really are, as your creation, so much alike. Yet, sometimes I feel like I am the worst sinner of them all. How truly amazing is Your love that You would love me. I am so unworthy, yet, I am tired of living in condemnation. Help me to live my freedom in You. I thank You, Lord, for another wonderful day. You are the best Valentine of all.

THE ONLY ONE

You're the only one who I can count on. You're the only one who knows my pain. You know the reasons for these actions of this heart of mine. You've been here. You've seen all the stuff that causes my mind to be jumbled up. You're the only one who won't let me down. You are forever faithful to this unfaithful heart.

You are the only one worthy of my love so help me to love You more. Let the expectations fall away on the ones around me for they will never live up to what You can do. They will always fail me one way or another. But, You never will.

You're the one who has the key to this cold heart. Open it up and let the rivers flow. Let Your tides of love and mercy wash over me. Let the fear and anger melt away so that I may be revealed in You.

You are the only one who knows what it takes to change this troubled mind. Set me free, oh free, indeed!

Journal Entry 2-5-06

This anger rages in me wanting to come out. Sometimes, I feel it will swallow me up, making me capable of anything. Why am I this way, Lord? I feel hate. I am so far from You, doubting everything. I know, I am selfish, Lord. I am full of self. I feel hopeless in my marriage, my salvation, myself. Will I ever come to the end of myself? I just don't care about anything. I'm so depressed and so miserable. I feel I just merely exist. Help me, Lord, I am helpless. I don't deserve any of Your blessings. Am I really Yours? Has this all been false assurance? I have no peace. My life is boring and meaningless. Marriage is not supposed to be this way. HELP ME!!!

EMOTIONS STIRRED UP

Evil and mean, that's what I can be. It comes from the depths inside of me. Anger it rages, unforgiveness it brews. Oh, how you wouldn't want to be in my shoes.

Emotions stirred up, telling me all kinds of awful stuff. I want to cry out ENOUGH, ENOUGH! Self-pity creeps in, just look where you've been. You deserve better, it isn't fair. I just want to run and go somewhere.

Away from myself, that's where I need to be. Into the arms of the One who saved me. Freedom and peace await me there. He can handle all that I can't bear.

Run fast, as fast as you can. He knows the places that I have been. Mercy and grace, He gives me then. Acceptance and love, that's what I receive, there's really no reason to grieve, for He has given me everything I need.

Emotions are calm, self-pity dies. Anger is gone. Jesus is here where I need Him to be, on the throne of my life, where He always should be!!

GOD'S HEART~

I KNOW

My Dear Child,

I know where you have been. I see your hurts. I do not hold it against you for your weaknesses. I put those weaknesses there so you would come to Me. I have the answers for your life. The answers rest in Me. Take one step at a time and learn to trust Me. You cannot change anyone but yourself. Let Me do the changing in others. Stop trying so hard and just let go of all that you know. I will take you places you have never been, places that only you and I can share. I have forgiven you! You are Mine and I am yours. Rest in this and nothing can shake you. I LOVE YOU, FOREVER!

Your Daddy,
God

Jeremiah 29:11(NLT) "For I know the plans I have for you, says the Lord. They are plans for good and not for disaster, to give you a future and a hope."

MY HEART~

Journal Entry 2-8-06

Lord, You are wonderful to me. I love You and truly want to live for You. I really want to reach out to others and be Your hands and feet. Thank You for my family. Although not perfect, they are mine. It is hard to keep focus on You. There are so many distractions. I'm tired of being blown about by the winds of life. I want to be firm and steadfast. Help me to do that. You have a mission for me: to reach the lost and to love You. I realize You want all of me. With the best that I can I give it to You. Forgive me for my sins, today. I have faith that You will change me from the inside out. Love You, Lord!

HIGHLY FAVORED

Highly favored I have been, from the beginning to the end.
Never have I gotten what I deserve. You have always known that I would be Yours.

Mercy You have given me, patiently waiting until I would see everything that I could be; A child of the King, chosen for all eternity.

I am Yours, You are mine. You have given me a love divine.
Unconditionally, forever faithful, a never-ending love.
Forever I will praise You for all that You have done!

Journal Entry 11-24-06

I am feeling like my old-self again, Lord. I am struggling inside so much. I need You to help me, Lord. My attitude has been sinful. I almost got more pain pills. I don't want to do these things. I am depressed about my weight. I hate being fat. Oh Lord, You are still my Father whether I am good or bad. I am still loved greatly by You no matter what my actions. Lord, I need to hear from You. I need You to refresh me once again. May I wake up tomorrow with a better attitude and outlook. Help me to be content. You have blessed my life so much and I am so thankful for that. I pray for the rest of my family to be saved. Help me to be a light. I thank You, Lord, for hearing me and answering me.

MIGHTY

In my own strength, I am powerless. My flesh is so weak. It cries out for the things that God hates. Oh, how I must depend utterly on the Holy Spirit to strengthen me. Every day I am faced with choices to make. Do I please myself or God?

Sometimes I don't even realize the war that rages within me. I am a threat to the enemy. He knows the power I have through Jesus. If he can keep me distracted and feeling defeated, then, he knows, I will be useless. Well, I am learning your strategy Satan. You have NO AUTHORITY HERE. Jesus Christ reigns in me and that makes me a MIGHTY WARRIOR! Satan, BEWARE!

GOD'S HEART~

IF YOU COULD ONLY SEE

My Dear Child,

If you could only see yourself the way that I see you, then, you would understand why I had to come and die for you. You are My Beloved Child. I created you. Before your parents even had you in mind, you were on My mind. You are woven into My divine plan. Oh, the plans that I have for you. They are wonderful, unimaginable plans. I have a specific work for you to do. To do that work, you must put your trust in Me. Put your life into My mighty hand. Release all that you hang onto and cling to Me.

I love you with an unfailing love! It will never go away, hurt you, let you down, or lead you astray. I want to be your all. I want to be your best friend who will walk with you every step of the way. All you have to do is COME and keep coming. Even when you mess up, come back again!! My mercy and grace are always there. I love you My child, now and for all eternity!

Your Daddy,
God

Matthew 11:28-29(NIV) "Come to me, all you who are weary and burdened, and I will give you rest. Take my yoke upon you and learn from me, for I am gentle and humble in heart, and you will find rest for your souls."

MY HEART~

Journal Entry 1-28-08

Well, Lord, I feel You have given me some direction in regards to my marriage. I just don't see any way possible for us to be together, now. It seems You have closed the door to protect me and my kids. Lord, bring the right people into my life and protect me further from bad influences that could come my way. I do ask You now, Lord, for when the time is right, you would bring a good man of Your Word into our lives. Bring someone who loves You and whom I could have a truly honest and trusting relationship with. I don't want to be single again, forever. Guide me day by day, Lord. I am so weak and I need help me with my many addictions. Help me to be truly free of them. I love You. You are still my God.

Journal Entry 3-11-08

My heart is breaking inside for all that is happening. My marriage really is over. As angry as I get, inside I am still sad. I'm not sure where to go from here. It's just You and me, God. I'm trying hard not to feel alone, but I do. I know You are here and love me. I wish I could feel You, touch You, and have You hug me. I want to love You more and more, Lord. Change this heart and life of mine. I do ask for another chance to have a relationship. Bring me a healthy, stable man who absolutely loves You first and foremost, please!!! I truly, in my heart, have always wanted that. If it's not Your will, so be it. You are in control. I love you, God, Jesus, and Holy Spirit.

FAITH

In this deep, dark place I cannot hear You or find You. I cry out, 'Lord, help me!' Why can I not hear You? Direct me, for I know not the way. Yet, still I have confusion, worry, and stress. Why is this so when I cry out? Where are You, Lord? Do You still love me? I cannot take one step forward! To the left or to the right, which path do You want for me?

Faith, faith is the key I read today; Release your faith in Me! Your faith is feeble and weak, but it is still there for I have given everyone their own measure of faith. I am growing your faith in Me. Have faith when you cannot hear Me. Have faith when you cannot feel Me. Have faith, My Child. I am still your God, leading the way even when you don't realize it. I am often a hidden God for the very purpose to help you release your faith. HAVE FAITH MY CHILD! That is the key! Then you will begin to see ME!!!

Journal Entry 10-20-2009

As I sit here on this day, I feel numb inside. This is something that I am quite used to feeling. I realize that everything I have done over the years: the pills, the pot, the constant overeating, whatever overindulgence I do, it is to cover the pain. Or, at least that is what I have been told over the years. Or, perhaps it is just the sin nature in me constantly warring against what is good. All I know is that I don't know how to live any other way in my life. I am so tired of this constant struggle in my soul. I realize that I must make a choice: continue on this path, which leads nowhere, or to step out and really change my ways. In doing so, I am choosing You, God, and Your ways. From the moment that I cried out to You on my bed, my thinking began to change. The problem is that I have had a hard time putting my faith into action. I am so tired of doubting if I am Yours. I want true peace in my heart. I have claimed to be a Christian for all these years, but why do I struggle so much to live it out? I constantly choose things that are killing me on the inside and harming my relationship with You, Lord. I cannot go on in my own strength, Lord. You know right where I am. I realize what I must do. For once, I am going to try my best to trust Your way. I need You to do for me what I cannot do for myself. I need You to carry me through the dark days of transition. Deep down, inside of myself, I am scared. There has got to be more for me in life than what I am living now. I want You, Lord, to open the doors of endless possibilities for me. To do things in my life which I never imagined. I want to be a person blown by Your Spirit, going wherever You lead. In my heart, I want this, but it seems so far from where I am now. Help me, Lord, in my weakness. Forgive me for my sins for they are so great. Every day, I sin against You. Humble my heart, Lord, and make it clean. Oh, how I long to be clean and feel clean before You. Give me a vision for my life. I praise and thank You, my Heavenly Father, for all You have given me, and for watching out for me. I have not deserved an ounce of mercy, yet everyday You give mercy to me. Even while watching me live in my sins. Blessed is the man who sins do not count against him. I am blessed, for You do not count them against me. That is the truth. Live in it, Connie!!!

Journal Entry 10-22-09

Tonight, I am praising You, God, for the fact that You hear our prayers. I rejoice that You hear my prayers. Oh, if I could just get that truth in my heart, that You have heard every feeble cry out of my mouth. You know my heart, even though it is so covered up to me. All I see and feel are mistakes and sins. I feel dirty most of the time. Although, the truth of the matter is, I am washed clean by the blood of Jesus Christ. It is the constant giving in to my fleshly cravings. If I am dead to sin, but alive in Christ, why do I sin so easily? Why do I feel so far from You? How I long to be able to just depend on You completely. How I need a move from You in my life. A big one so that I cannot mistake that it's You. Every day, I need reminders that You are so very near to me, that You long to be my companion on this journey in life. Please Lord, help me to see You, feel You, and just KNOW! I praise You even in the pit that I have myself in. I need You to lift me out and stand me on firm ground. Help me to change my life and my ways. Show me new paths and exciting transitions. May Your will be truly done in my life despite myself.

11-3-2009 Answered prayer! God brings Pastor Willie Miller into my life.

IS IT POSSIBLE

Is it possible that you could be the one?
Could you be the one that this heart has been praying for?
Is it possible that you could be the one?
The one I can give my whole heart to without reserve.
Is it possible that you could be the one?
The one that God will use to love me as Christ Himself loves me.
Is it possible that you could be the one?
The one I have dreamed of and desired since being a little girl.
Is it possible that you could be the one?
The one I can shower with all the love that I have to give.
Is it possible that you could be the one?
The one that I can live the rest of my days here on earth with.
The one that I can serve the King of Kings and Lord of Lords with?
Is it possible that you could be the one?
YES, because my God say's, "ALL things are possible with Him."

01-22-10 Willie and I were married! It's a new beginning. The new path that I prayed for has begun.

IN YOUR EYES

In Your eyes, I see my future,
a future so full of love and God's presence.
In Your eyes, I see a man,
a man that has been hurt and bruised and come out on the other side serving His God passionately.
In Your eyes, I see such emotion.
Emotion ready to be given to the one he loves-ME!
In your eyes, I see such passion.
Passion for the people around him, God's lost children, and most of all, passion for His God!
In your eyes, I see a man ready to be
loved as he deserves with no reserve. Touched, caressed, and kissed with love and tenderness.
In your eyes, I see my man.
The man I have been waiting for all these years. The man that God prepared for me to help heal all the hurt in my heart and to love me as God loves me.
In your eyes, I see everything!!!
Everything I need, want, and desire.
In your eyes, I am lost. I am lost in your tenderness and sweet caress. In your eyes, that is where my future is. I love you!

MY HEART~

Journal Entry 3-25-10

Wow, so many changes since I last journaled. Lord, I want to praise and thank You for all You have done for me. You have heard my cry and given me a wonderful gift. Finally, after years of heartbreak and feeling I can't be happy with a man, You have shown me that I can. You brought me the most wonderful man. Willie is amazing! You picked such a perfect man for me. I see, now, how marriage is supposed to be and how fulfilling it is when You are in it. Never could I have picked such a man for myself. I am so happy inside and content with him. I trust for the first time in my life. I know he does not want to hurt me. You have shown Your love for me through him. How perfectly You love me. How You long to give all the best things in this life to me. Thank You my Father God. No matter how long You allow me to have this gift of Willie, I will always be thankful that I have experienced true, Godly love.

Also, Lord, forgive me for my lack of faith at times in what You can do through me and in this church. I thank You that You have put me in this position of First Lady. At times, I feel myself not wanting it, but that is wrong. I have got to start seeing myself as You see me. You want to use me if I would just allow You to. I feel so unprepared at times for all this. I know You want to work through me. Help me to love these people that You have placed in my life. To see them as You do. Lord, I ask You to use me tonight through this women's fellowship. Help the dreams I have had of speaking become a reality. Help me to preach the Word smoothly and effectively to the people You send my way. I love you, Lord! I thank You over and over for blessing my life so much. You truly are a good and kind God. I love You!

Journal Entry 6-20-2010

The struggle deep inside me is crying out. It's been two weeks since I took one of those nasty pain pills. I want to be free from it, but it calls out. Oh, God, can I really do this? I want to, but how? How do I stay free? You have given me everything I need, yet it never seems enough. It is not going to be enough to just give up this or that. I need, God, for You to reveal to me the heart of the issue. For You to help me really deal with what's going on inside of me. I am asking You to do this on this day, June 20, 2010, please! Set me free, God. I am tired of this pull, this half-hearted way of life. I want Your passion in my life. I truly do, Lord. Show me Your ways, God, for they are not mine. God, I ask you to please keep me from going back. No matter what it takes, I know I have to do this. I need to so much. I need to trust You more than I ever have. Show me what it means to be free. I want to be free, Lord! You have given me a wonderful man that loves me and with whom I can serve You. Yet, I am so unworthy of the call. More and more, I feel unworthy. I hurt so deep down inside and I don't know why. I have no reason to not be happy. You have blessed my life so much and it's as if I take it all for granted. You say to call Your name and You will be there. I am calling, my Lord. Give me all that my heart can hold. I do feel alone in my sadness. I am tired of doing it on my own. I need You so much to carry me, to equip me. Take me to the place of deep trust that I see You take other people. Show me how and take me there. Give me the desire to want to go deeper into You because right now I do not want to.

Journal Entry 07-01-10

I don't know where to begin in my feelings, Lord. I feel sad and lost in this new land. It has been almost a month now that I have been without my "crutch" (pain pills) and I can't say that I exactly like how I feel. Oh, how I need You to do a new work in me, Lord. I still feel as if I just exist. How I need You to move in my life. I need to hear from You directly every day. I need to feel You and know You are there. I know in my heart and mind You are there, but sometimes it's so hard to feel You. I feel depressed inside and almost hopeless but, I know life is not hopeless! I am so overwhelmed with all the changes that have happened in my life and that are in the process of happening. I know You are in control and that You have a plan for me. I desire to do Your will but at times I sure don't act like it. I battle all these emotions and feelings.

I am torn about my girls. I hate that I am so far away from them, but, at the same time I know that this is where I need to be. I feel they don't know me or my heart's intentions. I let my girls down in many ways. I know I can't change the past and I need forgiveness from them. Lord, they need to know You so much. I am pleading on their behalf. Invade their lives with Your love. Save them and give them new life.

I don't know, Lord; I wish I felt happier and better. I have no reason to feel down. I have such a great man and the love he has given me is so amazing. You knew how I needed him and to know a love like this, a love that You lavish on me. How I long to just go and be with You, to live in Your paradise. This life has nothing to offer. Help me to not love this world any longer, but to love You with passion. Please! I need to know You better so I may help others know You. I want Your presence in my life. Despite my flesh, my spirit wants You. I love You, Lord Jesus, Holy Spirit, and Father God. Be my all!

GOD'S HEART~

I HEAR

My Dear Child,

The love you have for Me is so alive! Live in it, Connie. Don't doubt that I am here lifting you, hearing your every cry. I have given this man to you so I can love you through him. I want you to physically know the love that I have for you, My Child. I will restore the years Satan has stolen from you. That is My promise to you. You are beginning to see that restoration happening. Now, trust Me for more. One step at a time, one second at a time. Just trust and rest in My love for you. I love you with an everlasting, unfailing love. It will take time to get used to living in a new way, but don't quit now. I will take you to the secret place. In the secret place you can sit on My lap and feel My arms around you. I will love you like I did when you were just that little girl who was scared and feeling abandoned. I watched over your every step then, and I am doing it, now. I have not been mad at you all these years. Just sad and broken-hearted at what I have had to watch you doing to yourself. My love for you has never stopped. I have such plans for you My Child. I will make those plans come alive and you will know that you know it is Me who did it. Stand up, strong and tall with the purpose of spreading My love to others. Let My presence and My love be your motivation. Each day, when you are feeling weak and low is when you must come to Me. Allow Me make you strong. You cannot do it alone. In your strength, you will fail, but, in Mine, you are an overcomer. Walk into victory, My Child. It is yours and these chains no longer have to be on your feet. I sent My Son to set you free. Scream you are free, Connie. Free to serve Me, free to love as I have loved, and free to live with a new freshness in all that you do. Keep your eyes on Me and abide in My love. Recognize when you are weak and come to Me for your strength. I cannot help you if you do not let Me. Reach out to others. Write the passion I have given you and it will be used for My glory. I love you! Trust is allowing yourself to fall backward into the goodness of who I am. Trust Me fully!

Your Daddy,
God

1 Peter 5:10(NIV) "And after you have suffered a little while, the God of all grace, who has called you to his eternal glory in Christ, will himself restore, confirm, strengthen, and establish you."

MY HEART~

Journal Entry 7-26-10

I feel like I could explode inside, Lord. God, please help me to get out of this state of mind. It's horrible. I feel miserable inside: depressed and unsatisfied although I have no reason to feel this way. Jesus, I should be thankful for this home but sometimes I feel I am going stir crazy in this little place. Oh, how I wish I could just get away from myself. I just want to focus on losing this weight. I feel like starving myself. I'm tired of all these things controlling me. I'm wallowing in self-pity, forgive me, Lord. Help me to change this poor attitude of mine. I just don't feel like I am worth anything at this point. Why did you call me to be a pastor's wife? I am so unqualified for this. Willie is so different from me. Sometimes, I feel he deserves way better than me. I often wonder if he will really stay. Will he get tired of me and leave one day? Oh Lord, I am so unworthy of all this and, yet, You have blessed me. Thank You! You deserve my all. Help me to give my all.

Journal Entry 8-8-2010

"I have better for you" is what You spoke that day driving away from Mike's. I remember how lost and discouraged I felt inside wondering if it really was Your voice I heard. It was! Now, I see Your words fulfilled in my life. You have given me a man that is so much better than I could have imagined. So many years I spent in misery. So much hurt, confusion, and wondering if love could really be good; and, thinking that it was my entire fault, always wondering why I could not be happy in the relationship. You have shown me that the kind of love that You have created is real and can be perfect in Your sight. Thank You so much, Lord, for this man, Willie. I see all my imperfections, but he sees the woman that I am inside, the one that You see. I don't know how You put such a love in this man for me, but I am so glad You did. It has to be Your Holy Spirit loving me. Oh Lord, help me to be the wife this man deserves and the Godly wife I should be. Work in my heart and help our love to grow and protect our marriage. May you use us, Lord, as a living testimony to the world of Your redeeming love and that You do renew and restore what the enemy steals. I thank You, Jesus. I love You and I love this man You have given to me.

GOD MOVES US TO TEXAS

MY HEART~

Journal Entry 9-9-2010

I want to trust You like I have never trusted You before. I want all that You have for me. You have seen my fears, my concerns, and I am giving them to You to work them out. Even though I go on this new journey to Texas afraid, I go anyway because I know You will be with me. Help me to do what I cannot do on my own. I ask You to reveal new things to me and change this heart. I am tired of thinking negatively. I want to believe Your promises and really stand on them. Help me to not be afraid to really work for Your Kingdom. Give me the strength and energy I need. I ask You to protect my children and do a mighty work in their hearts. I know You will bring them around to You because You did it for me. You took care of me in all my foolishness and sinfulness. You waited, patiently, until the day I would be Yours. I want to fall in love with You, Jesus. Really love You! Holy Spirit, You have been my guide and often I have ignored Your leading, You're tugging at my heart. Thank You for living in me and producing in me a faith-filled heart. I love You, Father God, Son, and Holy Spirit.

Journal Entry 12-1-2010

It is amazing at what You are doing, Lord. In all my fear and worries, You have put me in the place that You have made just for me. Oh God, I long to feel You in a new way, to be free of these cravings of my flesh. I just cannot continue in the old ways because my position is too important. I have lives that I am influencing and I know You will hold me more accountable to living to the truth of Your Word. I thank You, Lord, for all that You have done in my life and where You have taken me through the years. I know You are faithful and I love You, Jesus. Show me more of who You are and what You want me to do. I know I need to repent of the negative attitude that I often have. Help me in my weakness. I cannot do ministry without Your Holy Spirit taking over. I need You to possess my very being. Please do this for me, Jesus. Give me the power that so many others have received. I want it, too. Help me to be genuine and real to others and to not hide in myself. I don't need what is comfortable, anymore. I need to step out and be uncomfortable. God, somehow, someway, use me in my weakness to show others Your love. Give me the heart that You have for the lost. Give me the heart that You have had towards me all these years. You see what I can be and what I am becoming; instead of, my sinfulness. Thank You for that. I don't have to continue in my old ways, anymore. You can show me new ways. Do that, Lord. I want to be totally free. I am already free. I just need to embrace my freedom and let go of what I hold on to so tightly. I love you, Lord. Thank You for all my life, the good and the bad that have come. You have been here every step of the way. I want to serve You more than anything, but I find that my carnal desires get in the way. I so easily give into them. There is a constant battle within myself between doing Your will and my own will. It feels like the battle will never end, but, then I remind myself that when I reach my heavenly home with You, there will be no more battle raging inside of me. Oh, what a day that will be when I come home to You, God. Thank You, thank You, and thank You for all my blessings. I am home here in Texas. It feels good even though I am so far from my girls. I trust You will take care of them. I am forever going to praise You for all the answered prayers. You have heard my cry. You are an awesome God. Thank You!!!!!

SELF

If I could get off the throne of my life, I would find peace; self is the real problem. Yes, I have an enemy in Satan. But I can fight him because he is someone outside of me. Where can I run to get away from myself? Self, desires my way, my time, and my things! It's all about ME! What a battle everyday to not wallow in my selfish wants and desires. Even in doing God's work, there I am, trying to creep in. Oh, how I get tired of this old self. It needs to die; to be crucified with my Savior. Just when I think I have it nailed, it comes back, again. This is the human problem: SELF! God leaves it up to us, this one part, to subdue self. Day in and day out: It is a choice, a decision, a stand, I must make consciously. So, when I see others thinking of their 'self', why am I surprised? Why am I offended? Why do I get angry? For, the very struggle I have, with me, is the one that they have, too. Praise God, I can have victory over me, if even for just this moment. One day, when I see my Savior face to face, the battle will no longer be raging within me. I WILL BE FREE!!!!!!

Journal Entry 4-11-2011

Lord, how I thank You for bringing Willie and I to Texas. What a journey this has been, Lord. Thank You for assigning this position to me. Seeing all You have done has built my faith, but yet, still I need my faith built more. I lack so much. I want to totally trust You and not worry. God, I ask You to continue to bless our ministry. I am sorry that I step ahead of You at times and try to fix things the way I think they need to be fixed. It never works. So many things could happen and I find myself getting lost in 'what ifs.' I love where You have put me. How hard it's been to make this huge move, but what blessings have come from it. I don't know why You chose me for this, but I'm so glad You did. Help me to become more like You, Jesus. Help me to really love like You. Forgive me for where I still have not totally given things to You. Help me to fully surrender. I want to be free of bondage to food and the desires that are still there, at times. I can feel myself getting consumed with being thin, but I know being thin will never make me truly happy. Even still, I want to feel good about how I look with the weight that I am. Help me to get to a healthy goal weight and never go back to being obese. Thank You for my life, for loving me, and for dying for me. You are my Father. I desire peace through You. I love You.

GOD'S HEART~

CHOSEN

My Dear Child,

Many are called, but few are chosen. Will you step up to the call? Will you give it all for Me? Do not let fear control you. Release it all to Me. I have appointed this position for you. It was not by chance that I chose you. Do not doubt what I can do through you. I know you are weary of the unknown road ahead. Do not look through your own eyes, for they will only see a short distance. Look through My eyes of amazing majesty and how I have woven you into My plan. A plan that is better than yours ever could be. Do not look at what is not there, but what can be through My power and might. You are intricately designed like no other; and, no other can fulfill what I have made for only you to do. I am working changes into the very center of your being, making you more like Me. This inner war is just the battle that has always been: your flesh fighting the spiritual. You cannot fight against the powers of this world. Let Me do the fighting for you, the changing you cannot do. You grow weary in your own strength. My Child, I will carry you. Trust Me in all you do. I will make you a mighty warrior, growing My Kingdom. So, relax, sit back, and see what I WILL do in your life.

Your Daddy,
God

1 Peter 2:9(ESV)   "But you are a chosen race, a royal priesthood, a holy nation, a people for, God's OWN possession, so that you may proclaim the excellencies of Him who has called you out of darkness into His marvelous light."

MY HEART~

Journal Entry 6-5-2011

Oh my, Lord, so much You want to do in me and through me. Father, my heart desires to serve You and be a vessel, but it's not 100%. It's like I hold onto just a little bit for myself. Why can I not just fully give You my all? Help me to trust You. Help me to be teachable. This road You have chosen for me is harder than I've ever known; and yet, more fulfilling than anything in this world. You are what it's all about, not me. I have failed so many times and my sins are great; yet, You use me. How merciful You are, my Lord. How gracious, loving, and patient You are. Jesus, I need You to consume me. Help me to die more and more. Connie is fighting to stay alive; but I can't let her. Because in staying alive, I really die. I want my life to be in You; and yet, I don't. But You are bigger than me, God. I give You permission, today, to do whatever it takes, to make me willing to give my all to You. I need You to do what I cannot. I need You to help me love people. I mean *truly* love them.

Lord, I am petrified to visit this women's prison and give my testimony. I know I have to do this. I know You have a purpose for sending me. I know You will use me. God, I ask You to direct me. Show me what to say. Help me to get out of the way so You can come forth. I want to be used by You in such a big way, to do what my calling is. I need You or I will fail. So many people need to know of Your love. I know You have given me a gift of writing. I ask You to give me a gift of speaking as well. As I see my husband up there preaching, I see how You use him so mightily. He is my Pastor, as well as my husband. I want to be used, too. I know there is a price, a sacrifice to pay. But it will be worth it.

Oh, how You have never given up on me. You still don't. Help me to not give up on myself. Help me to not give up on Your people, to know there is always hope.

Journal Entry 6-12-11

I don't understand how I can go from faith to so much doubt. Lord, this past weekend was emotionally horrible. All that I thought I believed, I am questioning. I am questioning You, Lord. Do I really trust anything about You? How can I be used if I can't even go through a healing line? I know I have a trust problem with You. Maybe I have not believed at all. I am so scared to follow You. Why can't I just give my all? What keeps holding me back? I don't understand why it's so hard to lay aside what holds me down. The anger and rebellion, that rose up in me this weekend, I did not expect. God, am I really Yours? Why do I struggle so? I just want to give up. It's too hard to do this. I don't know why I jumped on going to the prison so eagerly. I have nothing to offer the ladies in this prison. The thought of standing and speaking in front of them and giving my testimony brings such feelings of unworthiness. What good am I to them if I can't even trust You? How can I go before them and speak of You when I have doubted, ran, and struggled so much all these years? Especially, when I doubt everything, I thought I believed. I have no power, Lord! I need Your Holy Spirit and unless You touch me somehow, I cannot go forward. I need a touch from You that I know is from You! I need Your reassurance somehow, someway. No man can give it to me. Only You can. I am sorry for how I've been acting and my disobedience. What more can I say? You know the horrible thoughts and doubts I have had towards You. But You can handle it, right? At least, that's what people say. I have a lot of bitter feelings. I can't live up to all that You require. You say if I don't obey, then I don't love You. Well, I feel like I have never loved You. When have I obeyed? Do I please You in any way? My mind is so messed up. I needed that healing last night but pride, rebellion, and fear got in the way. There is such a price to pay, a sacrifice to make to follow You. I can't seem to muster up any boldness or courage to do as You require. I am so tired of these thoughts; the emotional prison I have myself in. I can't unlock the door. Is it too late for You to unlock it for me?

PRISON WALLS

I am in a prison, but this prison has no bars. I have no key to unlock it myself. This prison has held me for so long. Oh, how I long to be truly free from my own self-made walls. The prison of my thoughts and emotions is so strong. Some days, I feel there is no escape. Jesus, You say, 'You have come to set the captives free (Luke 4:18).' Well, this captive needs You to unlock the cell; but, most of all, to keep me from returning. In some ways, these prison walls are comforting. They are all I know. If I step outside too far, life gets overwhelming. I want to go back to what I am used to. But there is no freedom there. I must choose to walk through the cell door that Jesus has unlocked. I cannot look back. I must take one step at a time as Jesus holds my hand and directs me. I must keep my eyes directly on Him because He say's, "With Him, I can do all things (Philippians 4:13)." So, I step outside the cell door, slam it, and let Jesus throw away the key. Then, freedom will come. Fear will leave and I will become what He wants me to be.

GOD'S HEART~

I CAN HANDLE IT

My Dear Child,

You asked Me if I could handle your honesty. Have you forgotten that I know every part of you? I know every thought and motive that is in your heart and mind. I even know why you feel the way you do and why you struggle so much. There is nothing secret to Me. I created your very being. You don't have to hide or pretend when you doubt and are discouraged. Voice your feelings to Me. Let them out so I can do a work in you. I want to heal every hurt that you have. I want to soothe you with My unconditional love. Nothing you say will surprise Me.

My Child, no matter what emotions, doubts, and fears you have; I am bigger than all of it. I can handle what you can't. What I need, for you to do, is just trust Me. I know it is not always easy for you to do that. But, because I love you so much, I will not let you be comfortable inside until you trust Me with even the littlest of details. I want to move you into what I have for you. I want to do in you, and through you, what you could never do on your own. You will have times of wrestling with your own will and Mine. That's ok, because through that you will find that My perfect will is what you need. It's for the good. All of it!

I am patient, My Child. I know that your heart desires to serve Me. What I want you to learn is that more importantly than serving Me, I want you to just spend time with Me! Allow My love to surround you. I want you to know I will never let you go! I will never give up on you. I will not forsake you! Let Me love you! Then, you will be strong enough and bold enough to share My love with others. You must be filled up with My Spirit, but first, you must empty yourself to Me. You must talk to Me and trust Me. I know you will have times of falling down.

But, every day, you trust Me more and more. I am working in you always. So, be reassured, My Child; I can handle your honesty. I love you no matter what!

Your Daddy,
God

2 Corinthians 12:9(ESV) "My grace is all you need. My power works best in weakness." So now I am glad to boast about my weaknesses, so that the power of Christ can work through me."

MY HEART~

RESCUE ME

Your grace is intertwined throughout my whole being. When I am at my worst, Your grace is at its strongest. You save me from myself, which is what I need to be saved from the most. My ways, my thoughts, my actions are independent from You. I was not made to be independent, but totally dependent on You. My life is a process of letting go of that independence. Sometimes, I hold on so tightly to my wants and desires. This does not work. I need You so desperately to come and rescue me from me. Rescuing me is exactly what You do. You want to rescue me every day of my life. You want to pick me up and set my feet on the right path, the right direction. You love me so much. You hate to see the dark places that I go on my own. You are the parent who is reaching out their hand to the helpless child; but the child lets go of the hand that You offer and, sometimes, does not take it at all. It saddens Your heart to see this. You see the whole picture of where the independence from You will lead. It involves pain, desperation, and torment! So, You wait ever so patiently for me to come to my senses. You wait until I am so tired and exasperated and I cry out to You: 'Father help me!' You come running to me! You want to rescue me. That has been Your desire all along. Like Prince Charming, the one I used to dream of when I was a little girl. You would do anything to have my love and affection. You would go to the ends of the earth to search for me. You are better than that Prince Charming. You are my Father, my Daddy, my Creator, my Friend, and my very Sustainer of life. You wanted to rescue me so badly from myself that You sent Your only Son. That is how deeply You care! How deeply You see the mess that an independent life from You will be. You want to sweep up that mess and make me clean through Your Son's shed blood on the cross. One room, at a time, of my hurts, disappointments, and failures; You will clean and make new, if I let You. That is the key- letting You. Even if it's a halfhearted willingness, that's all You need. For, You will make it whole-hearted once I see what You can do. So, I say, 'Yes! Come and rescue me from me!

Journal Entry 9-21-2011

Well here I am again, Lord. So much has happened since I turned 42. You have done so much in me. Some days, I feel it strongly and other days, I don't recognize it at all. You have been faithful and I thank You for that. You are so patient with me.

I can't believe how much weight I have lost. It has been a long, hard road, but well worth it. I never want to go back to being obese. Help me to keep working out and have balance in all areas of my life. Change me more, Lord. I love You, but I don't feel like writing anymore right now.

Journal Entry 4-24-2012

Thank you, my Daddy, for getting me home from Nicaragua safely. I appreciate my family and home so much. I do, but I feel the battle already raging in me. My eating and my fleshly desires are becoming stronger and stronger. I know that it is You I need, Daddy. Please, meet me in my need and help me in my weakness. Help me to get re-focused on You. Holy Spirit, I need Your thoughts. Mine are overtaking me, Daddy. I am so weary of giving this presentation on Sunday. I am totally uncomfortable speaking in front of people. I need You to give me Your words and what You want me to say. Help me to be bold and sure of myself. I thank You that You love me in my weakness.

Help me and help my girls to get out of the pit. I ask You to move mightily on their behalf. Have mercy on them and reveal Your mercy to them. Open their eyes! Give them Your thoughts. Send Your servants to be a witness to them. Help them to recognize it's You. Do it, Lord, in Your timing and in Your way.

I love You, my Daddy. You are ever so patient with me. You do lead me and have mercy when I fall. I need You to hold me up. Keep me from the pit of despair and sin. Help me to not be shaken, but to be confident in You! I love You, Father God!

AND THE BATTLE RAGES ON

Deep inside, there's a war going on. From the moment I awake, and sometimes, even while I sleep, it calls me to do all the things that take me far from You. This flesh wants everything opposite that You want for me. So, Your Spirit fights for me. You are constantly reminding me that You must have control. You are stronger. But You allow me to contend with my flesh. I wrestle back and forth. For if there were no wrestling, there would be no joy in the victory. You allow me to choose whom I will serve: my flesh or Your Spirit. You allow me to discover that I can subdue this flesh. One battle at a time I come to learn that I must deal quickly and decisively with this flesh. If I do not, my flesh will win. Just one thought, of giving in, soon becomes two and, then, three and, all of a sudden, it has taken me. My thoughts become the act. How I wish this battle would end; to get rid of the constant struggle that rages inside me. Then, You remind me; that, the very war that's going on is the evidence that I am Yours. I was dead in my sins before I received Your saving Grace, and You came to live in me. Dead things have no war to win. I had no choice but to follow this flesh and the evil desires that it wanted. But, then, You came and set Your home inside of me. Your mercy and grace have allowed me to have a choice. You give me the strength to win. You help me to see that my flesh is crucified with Christ. Now, it is Your Spirit that gives me life. You, also remind me that until my fleshly body dies, I will always have to contend with it wanting control. So, I need to get the strongest weapon that I have, which is Your written Word. I need to get it into my mind, my heart, and do what it says. That is how I win! I must train my flesh to obey Your Spirit that lives in me. The training will be painful. But, in the pain, You will make me more like You. So, as I awake another day and, I feel the battle raging on, I can be assured I have all I need to come out victoriously.

Galatians 5:16-18(ESV) "But I say, walk by the Spirit, and you will not gratify the desires of the flesh. For the desires of the flesh are against the Spirit, and the desires of the Spirit are against the flesh; for these are opposed to each other, to prevent you from doing what you would. But if you are led by the Spirit you are not under the law."

GOD'S HEART~

YOU CAN BE FREE

My Dear Child,

Step into what I have for you. You can be free from the addictions in your life. They have no power over you anymore!! So much better waits for you, My Dear Child. I love you! I want the best for you. These things are not the best. You are trusting in something that can never fill the hunger you have. I want to take you deeper into Me. I will show you marvelous things to come. I have better things for you. My plans are great for you, My Child. TRUST ME to fulfill! New paths have been made for you, but you must take the step onto that path. Don't look back and feel you are missing something. You are not! It is a lie. The enemy of your soul wants to destroy the beautiful creation that I made in you. Take care of yourself and love yourself as I love you. These things are only destroying you and holding you back. You are Mine and I desire good things for your life. You can walk into the future with a new song in your heart and a stride in your step. Great things WAIT for YOU! TRUST IN ME! I will not fail you. I know you love Me. But you are trying to live in your own strength. You cannot do this. Let Me lead you and carry you when you are down and the road is hard. I LOVE YOU, MY CHILD! WALK FREE!

Your Daddy,
God

John 8:36(NLT) "So if the Son sets you free, you are truly free."

MY HEART~

Journal Entry 5-4-2012

I have been so far from You since coming back from Nicaragua. It seems at times that my life is falling apart. I guess that falling apart is not a bad thing. I see how I have hung to so many other things, but You. They are all failing, but You don't fail! I know You are working Your plan and will in my life. You are bringing me to the depths of myself. The pain is so real and deep. I feel the breaking beginning, Lord. I hate the dark periods of doubting. I feel I can get through anything if I just know I am Yours, that my faith is real no matter how small. Somehow, someway, will You confirm this to me for good? Please, Jesus! I need peace in this confirmation once, again! It's hard to deal with this. I suppose, I am working out my own salvation.

Journal Entry 5-5-2012

You heard my cry! You answered and I thank You for that. Through a stranger, You verified that I am Yours and I am to write my books!! There is no way he would have known that about me except by Your Spirit. He told me that the intercessor that lives in me was going to become loud and clear. Get ready to be on the forefront. How I needed this touch from You.

Oh, Lord, show me and give me supernatural strength to turn from my sin and rebellion. It needs to be all about You. No glory to me!!

AWAKENING

I feel an awakening going on inside of me. Things that I thought I understood were just a mere taste of who You really are. You are taking me so much deeper to the depths of Your love. Each new revelation, I am getting about who You really are, creates such a stirring deep within me. You are creating a passion that will never burn out. It is Your Holy Spirit inside of me working in the inner depths of my being. You are changing me one day at a time, one step at a time as I learn to walk in the reality of Your love and all that You did for me. For so long I have made it about what I can do to earn acceptance. When, all along, that acceptance has been there. Your love has never been like human love because human love is, often, conditional. Your love for me was there before I was even born. You sent Jesus to die for me before I had even breathed one breath or committed any sin against You. That is true love! You have watched over all my ways. In my darkness and helplessness, Your mighty hand has pulled me out of the quicksand of futility. I have purpose, now. I have a mighty, Daddy God who will never stop loving me, no matter what! I feel the chains, of all the lies I have believed for so long, falling off one link at a time, as I replace those lies with the truth of Your Word. You intended to create me and lavish Your love upon me. I am no mistake and You are working greatness in my life. I can feel that greatness, through You, coming forth like a whirlwind of fire. There is no stopping it because who can hold Your Spirit down? Not even my worst, rebellious day prevents Your plans from being fulfilled for my life. You are in control, even when I act as if I am the one running the show. Oh, how my heart longs for more and more of You. All the things I have chased after, day after day, can never fulfill me like You do. Help me to stay in that truth. Awaken me more, Sweet Jesus, to all that You died to give me. I want to rest from all my striving and totally lay it all at Your feet. I want all that You have for me even when that requires going through the pain of letting go of my self-made walls. My self-made walls really haven't protected me; instead, they alienated me from Your great Love. This love I so desperately need every day of my life and into eternity. The only love that can truly save me, the love that I was created for: a love relationship with my Daddy God!

Journal Entry 8-1-12

Jesus, I want to praise You and thank You for Your wonderful grace. How You are opening my eyes to so much. More and more, I am being set free. I have lived under condemnation for so long. Thank You for bringing me Joseph Prince's book, *Destined To Reign*. Your Spirit is revealing the truth to me. I have been Yours, all these years. I am sorry I have doubted You, Jesus.

I ask You to help me get rid of this sin in my life. Every day is a battle to not go to food for comfort and satisfaction. Help me to destroy the lies I believe. I thank You for all You are doing in me and, that no matter what, Your love will always be there. You will never leave me or forsake me. Help me to really believe that!

Journal Entry 9-7-2012

I'm at this place again of feeling fearful and far from You. I feel heavy inside and I doubt, again. Lord, who are You? What's real in all the things I hear preached from Your Word? I have felt You working in my life and heart, showing me Your love. There are so many people with so many different view points and people giving scripture to back it up. I don't want to be swayed with wrong teaching.

I have felt in my heart that what I have heard lately is really truth. Is it? I need Your Holy Spirit to show me truth. I don't want to take my sin lightly; but, I don't want to feel bad inside, anymore. Is Your love really constant? Do You want me to feel bad and broken inside? I want to feel good about You. I want to feel free to come to You, even when I deliberately sin. I want to give others compassion in their sin and doubt because I feel the doubt, at times, and have my own struggles with sin.

Was I wrong to feel as strongly as I did yesterday with the man, we had our meeting with? I hated the judgment he threw out so openly about the church. His judgment has stirred up anger in me. I felt it was wrong, not showing love. I don't want to be like that. It's Your love that draws me, not when I feel judgment. You took my judgment and I have no hope outside of You, Jesus. My heart truly believes in You. But, getting sin out of my life has been so difficult. I can't do anything without You changing me on the inside. There is more work to do. Show me where I am wrong. I don't want to teach the wrong thing.

Cover me until my mind is fully convinced of Your love, until I stop believing lies, until I stop being comfortable with my ways. Save me from myself. Help me to love. Lift me out of this and give me Your peace once again!

GOD'S HEART~

ACCEPTED RIGHT NOW

My Precious Child,

I see you! I am not mad at you. I want you to get that! I forgave you before you were even born. I knew how many times you would turn and run to your idols. You are still Mine. Even though it hurts Me to see you go through these periods of doubt, I know this is what you must go through to bring you fully to Me. Fully you will serve Me, love Me, and want Me. You desire Me more than you did yesterday and the day before that and so on. It does not look or feel that way to you, but I see your heart. Your heart is right because you received My Precious Son. It takes time for your actions to catch up with your heart. Trusting Me is what you must do. Completely trust Me! I am patient and I am working it all so that trust will keep growing. Look where I have taken you from already! You are growing! Don't compare that growth with anyone else. You are My individual child. I know how to grow you up. In love, I will help you. Remember, I am not mad at you. I accept you right where you are at.

Your Daddy,
God

Ephesians 1:4(NLT) "Even before he made the world, God loved us and chose us in Christ to be holy and without fault in his eyes."

MY HEART~

MY VALUE

Lord, help me to see my value. I know You are real and that You love me so much; and yet, every day I struggle to see the value that I have in Your eyes. I see all the walls that I have built around my heart; and, letting You tear them down is a scary and painful process. Just when I think that I am finally seeing myself as You do, and that my performance is not what matters, I slide back into my old way of thinking and coping. Yesterday's revelation of You is not good enough for today. I need a fresh touch and revelation from You everyday! Yet, I let myself live from a touch that You gave me months ago, and I don't seek that touch from You today. You truly are my Daddy because You only let me go so far and so long on my own choosing. Then, You pull me back with Your love strings. When I let go of You, and I feel that I have gone too far away this time, You do something that reminds me it was always You hanging onto me. I am never too far from Your reach and Your love. You are always encompassing me; especially, when I choose to do opposite of what You want me to do. Oh, how valuable I am to You. How valuable we all are to You and if we could just get that deep down in our hearts. When I look at myself and those around me, I see that is really one of the biggest reasons we choose sin over You. We allow ourselves to forget just how cherished and esteemed we are by You. We start to devalue ourselves which creates a cycle of devaluing those around us. We feel so horrible inside and, can't control our inner man, so, we try to control everything around us on the outside. Oh, how I need You to constantly remind me who I am. I am a precious Child of the Almighty, Creator, God! Forgive me for forgetting almost daily that Your Son paid a high price, death on a cross, to prove my value and worth.

Journal Entry 9-12-2012

I thank You, Lord, for my life. Thank You for always loving me. You have grown me so much and are healing me. I know I am just beginning on this road of understanding which is my coping patterns and the healing process. I ask You, Holy Spirit, to reveal more and more of Jesus to me. Help me to become steady and unwavering. I do recognize that, when things appear to be out of my control, I react in wrong ways. Break down the wall of distrust that is around my heart.

GOD'S HEART~

DOUBT

My Dear Child,

I see you in your doubt of the love that I have for you. I know that in your heart you want to believe with a faith that is unwavering, that my love will never go away. You try, and then, one word from someone else's doubt stirs up all the insecurities of the little girl in you that has felt abandonment and rejection. I know it seems too good to be true that I will never leave you nor forsake you. But, My Child, it is true! In My Word, I tell you that I have loved you with an everlasting love and that I have drawn you with loving-kindness. Think on that word: *everlasting*. It means that My love for you will never come to an end. NEVER! I have chosen to love you even when you are at your worst. When you are in your doubt and dark place that no one understands, I am there still loving you. Do you not think that I am even bigger than your doubt? My Child, it is Me who is carrying you and holding your very life in My Hand. I have sealed you with My Holy Spirit and nothing can snatch you out of My hand. The moment you received Jesus' sacrifice, on the cross for your sins, was the moment that I made you Mine for eternity. I am not like any human that has been in your life. Some have left you and rejected you, even when you were just that little girl wanting to be loved. What I need for you to do, when you are reminded of all that rejection and abandonment, is cry out to Me and not run. Open your heart to Me. Express to Me your pain and doubt. Let Me wash the pain away with My unending love. The enemy of your soul wants you to think that I am disappointed in you because of doubt. I am not! Your doubt does not surprise Me, nor does it stop Me from lavishing My love on you.

My Child, your performance is not what I see. You don't have to hold it all together on the outside when you are falling apart on the inside. Take the mask off and fall apart in My loving arms. It is when you fall apart and stop pretending that I can take you and mend all the torn pieces of your heart. I will replace that doubt with security. When you doubt, it does not mean your faith is not there. It is just hidden by the cloud of doubt. But that cloud will fade away as you begin to reach out to Me and see that I have been carrying you all along in my mighty hand. I love you, My Child, with an EVERLASTING LOVE!

Your Daddy,
God

Jeremiah31:3(NIV) "The Lord appeared to us in the past saying; I have loved you with an everlasting love; I have drawn you with loving-kindness."

MY HEART~

REDEEMING LOVE

Despite my sin and rebellion, You delight in redeeming me and doing good things for me. I have wasted so many years thinking You are angry and far from me. It has never been Your desire for me to be far from You. You have been here all my life. How Your heart must break at times while You have had to watch me try and figure out my own way in this life. Yet all the while, You were sending Your angels to fight on my behalf the war that I couldn't see. You have protected me and guarded me. When I have been lost in my struggle with this flesh, You are there in the unseen shadows of my life watching out for me. Now, I know that Jesus won the war for me before I was even born. You chose me and adopted me into Your Kingdom. I am a warrior, now, beginning to fight the good fight of faith. You are captivating me more every day with Your great love for me. You have been drawing me closer to your heart. As this is happening, you are re-making my cold heart; a heart that has built many walls of lies around it. The more I read Your wonderful Word, and as I experience Your loving desires for me, this cold heart is turning hot for You! You are burning away the lies and putting truth in me which is transforming me. I can no longer be who I was. The transforming that You are doing in me is through the power of Your living Word, sifting through my whole being, creating changes.

Sweet Jesus, I see now that You saved me the moment I cried out to You, but You want to do more than save me. You want me to experience You in this fleshly, mortal body. You have shown me that You are saving me from myself. As I learn more of your truth, the lies that I have believed, are dispelled. I can see that You are perfecting me. When the day comes that I leave this earthly body, Your work will be done in me. I will be with my Sweet Savior and I will be completely perfected. What a wonderful Savior You are!!!!

Psalms 107:2 (ESV) "Let the redeemed of the LORD say so, whom he has redeemed from trouble."

GOD'S HEART~

YOU ARE REEDEEMED

My Dear Child,

I am Your Redeemer. Do you realize what this means for you? This means you are totally accepted and forgiven. I have bought you back from the curse of sin. I paid the debt that you owed. I have restored you into right standing before Me. I have kept My new covenant promise, which is to no longer remember your sins. This is because you have trusted in what has been done for you through My Son Jesus' shed blood on the cross. He is the perfect sacrifice for the sins of all mankind. I heard you the day that your heart first came into agreement with Me, that you needed forgiveness. That moment is when you repented. When you acknowledged your need, for forgiveness from Me, is when I came to live inside of you and washed you totally clean.

You see, I did not wait for you to stop sinning before I saved you. There is no way you could have stopped sinning in your own strength. I redeemed you before you were ever born. I have done the work of your redemption, so stop striving for My love and just rest in it. I know that you will still sin and fall short, but even then, My fellowship with you is not broken. How can fellowship be broken with Me when My Son's blood is continuously washing you clean?

My Child, there are sins you commit every day without even realizing you are committing them. The moment you first confessed to Me your need for forgiveness, and believed My Son paid for your sins, was the moment your sins were gone: past, present, and future. You can still confess to Me when you know you sin and ask me to help you; but that is only so Satan cannot use your sin against you to make you feel as if you are unworthy of My love and forgiveness. If I required you to confess every sin that you did, or will do, to be forgiven, you would be confessing all day long. Your salvation would be dependent on your works and not what My Son has already done. So, My Child, lay down those things that you carry. I want you to rest in My perfect love for you. I have you covered all the way into eternity. You are REDEEMED!

Your Daddy,
God

Isaiah 43:1(NIV) "But now, this is what the LORD says-- he who created you, Jacob, he who formed you, Israel: "Do not fear, for I have redeemed you; I have summoned you by name; you are mine."

MY HEART~

Journal Entry 2-12-2013

Wow, Lord! You want me to go to Your high places so I will be able to receive power to pour myself out with utter abandonment in acts of self-giving. The only way to do this is to let go of the plans I have for my life and submit to Your plans for my life. This will take obedience. Obeying is something that I often fail to do. Oh, change my heart, Dear Lord. I am so full of me!

TREASURES IN THE DARK

As I walk through the dark places of my soul, God will show me who He really is. I will learn to trust Him in deeper and new ways. There are certain treasures that He wants to give me, but I can only find them as I go through the darkness. As I walk in this unknown place, at times, I will feel as if I am being swallowed whole. I do not have to be afraid. It is in the darkness that I will learn to recognize His voice more clearly. In the dark places of my soul, He will reassure me that He has called me by name. He may allow me to stumble, but He will not let me fall.

As we journey together through this darkness, others may not even notice that I am walking on this road. These are a few of the secret places that only God and I know about. When I am in this secret place with God, He will teach me things of great worth. He will bring me through this place of pain and give me riches I will never lose. I can hear Him beckoning me "Come, My Child! Wait no longer to do what must be done. Just enter in!"

Isaiah 45:3(HCSB) "I will give you the treasures of darkness and riches from secret places, so that you may know that I, Yahweh, the God of Israel call   you by your name."

LOSING MY LIFE

To really find my life, I must lose it. This doesn't make much sense when I think about that through my own reasoning. But then I am reminded by the Holy Spirit that my own reasoning is part of the life that I must lose. To really have life in the here and now, I must put on the mind of Christ daily. He is living in me and He is where I find true life. I must lose all the empty, vain imaginations that have dictated how I have lived my life. These are the empty, useless, life-sucking pursuits of this world that I have chased. To lose my life, I must take every thought I have captive and evaluate it. Is my thought "truth," according to what God's Word says, or is it a lie? I must allow the Holy Spirit to give His wisdom. He wants to give it and direct me, but I must be willing to lose the old life, my old self, which is full of sin and opposition to God. I must choose to lose the carnal mindset that is fixated on me: my wants, my desires, and my cravings.

To lose my life, requires me to admit my defeat. I cannot win this war against sin in my life. I cannot overpower the demonic influence that is all around me in my own human strength. I fail every time. I need the power of the One who created me.

To lose my life I am trading it for a much greater, unimaginable life. I am trading it for the supernatural life of Christ. As I lose my life He is allowed to come forth and use me. I become His way of being and doing in the earth. I, literally, become the conduit of His glory. That is amazing. He gives me new desires as I trade my life for His. As I walk these desires out, that He gives me, they truly satisfy because I am doing what He has purposed for me to do. I do not have to continue searching for the next thing that might finally satisfy me as I did in my old life.

As I lose my life, I receive power to overcome all opposition from the enemy. I am given authority over the enemy and he is, then, under my feet. He is no longer master over me for I have a new, loving master, Christ Jesus!

When I think of all these things, I can now see that losing my life is a wonderful thing. I can willingly lay down my life for Christ just as Christ laid down His life for me.

Matthew 10:39 (ESV) "Whoever finds his life will lose it, and whoever loses his life for my sake will find it."

Journal Entry 3-14-2013

Help me to get back to You, Lord. Get me out of myself and my mental torment. I don't like being here: all frustrated, discouraged, and feeling hopeless. I am feeling doubt and fear, again. I feel I am so far from you, again. I hate it. I am tired. I have been horrible this week sinning against You. I am sorry, Father. I need Your forgiveness. Every time that I chose sin, I am sacrificing intimacy with You because sin takes me away from You. Then, I have an open space for the enemy to get in. Help me to decide to be free of this bondage to food. Even writing this, I feel as if I am forcing it, and I feel as if You are mad. Please, despite my sin, revive me and give me hope, again. Help me to receive Your forgiveness. I need it. I need Your grace right now. Thank You for giving it to me, even though I don't feel it.

God, I am so discouraged with this church. When will it ever grow? How long will it be like this with little help and low attendance? I know my eyes are not on You, but it is so hard when week after week, lack of help and church attendance remain the same. Help me to see it differently and change my motives. Oh, how I hate when I get into myself so bad that I can see nothing else. I need to stay in Your love. Thank You for Your unconditional love.

GOD'S HEART~

FIXED ON YOU

My Dear Child,

I wish you could always remember how fixed I am on loving you. Unfortunately, your flesh is often weak and it overtakes you. Then, you begin the cycle of pulling away from Me, wondering how I could choose to love someone like you. My Child, these are not My thoughts towards you. I want to remind you that when I say I am fixed on loving you, this means, you are completely secure. I am immovable in your life. Before you were born, I fixed My love upon you. It was firm, in My mind, to love you with such passion that even when you sin against Me, turn your back on Me, and go your own way, I would not change My mind about you. I am fixed and unchanging in My love for you. You must remind yourself daily of this simple truth: I sent My One and Only Son to die for all the sins you would ever commit. When you do sin, you forget that it is no surprise to Me. It is because I fixed My love on you that you are allowed to be weak and fail. I don't want your perfection. My Son, Jesus, is that perfection for you. What I want is your independence from Me to decrease, and your dependence upon Me to increase. I love you, My Child. Remember, I AM FIXED on loving you!!

Your Daddy,
God

Romans 5:8(NLT) "But God showed his great love for us by sending Christ to die for us while we were still sinners."

MY HEART~

Journal Entry 3-17-2013

Oh, Lord, help me! I feel so full of self pity, anger, discouragement, impatience, and the list goes on. Show me where I am wrong. Holy Spirit, help me to change. I know You are here, but I feel so unworthy because I know I am not acting as I should. I am wrestling with You once again, Lord. I am looking through my own eyes. Show me how to love people, to truly love them as You do. I am so tired of getting frustrated with people and things I can't control. It consumes me sometimes. I thank You that, despite how I feel and act at times, You have blessed me.

GREAT DETERMINATION

How amazingly great Your love is for us. I try to comprehend it and it eludes me. As You bring new people into my life that You want me to love, You show me that the only way I can do it right is to look at how You love me. You love me with determination. You made up Your mind about me before I was even born. Once I was born, You were firm in Your intention to draw me to You and save me. You would not change your mind about me, no matter how I acted. You established a specific course of action to resolve the separation between us. That action was sending Your Son, Jesus, to die on a cross for me and all of humanity's sin and rebellion. At that point, it was settled. Your determination to love me into eternity would not stop. It doesn't stop, ever!!! You are fixated on not only saving me, but on blessing me and showing me favor all the days of my life. It has nothing to do with my performance, but for the plain and simple fact that You want to show me grace. You made a choice not to give up on me. When I keep all this in mind, I am able to love others with the same determination. When I am ready to not reach out anymore, because of one more hurt from someone, You remind me how many times I have hurt You. Yet, You did not turn away. When others are in the midst of despair, turning one more time to the very thing that is killing them, You remind me of the despair and futility I have gone through. I am reminded of the mercy and patience You have shown me while I was repeating my mistakes over and over, again. You show me the many common threads that we all have and that we really aren't that different from each other. We all have sinned and messed up time and time again. We all have tried to live life our own way, making for ourselves our little idols that take the place of where You should be in our lives. We all want unconditional love, acceptance, and to have a purpose. We have gone to many extremes to find love and acceptance. Some of us have found it thanks to Your awesome determination to chase us down with Your Mighty Love. We have a purpose now, which is to tell others about You. You are a wonderful, passionate God. You gave Your own Son's life to show how determined You were to give us eternal, abundant life!!!!

MY EVER CONSTANT

You are the constant in my ever-changing world. People come in and out of my life but You are here to stay with me. Oh, how badly I need to remember this. In a world where there are so many distractions, I need Your magnetic Presence pulling me toward You. I am easily drawn to and cling to everyone, and everything else, but You. When I allow myself to be drawn away from You, I am easily shaken and moved because You are the only un-movable, un-shakable rock that I can stand on. I was never meant to depend on things in this world. I was created to be utterly dependant on You because You are the one who made me. You know what I need and when I need it. You know the plans You have for me. These plans are great and mighty because You are the Great and Mighty God. I am Your child, created in Your image, so why should I expect any less of my life? You created me to do the impossible through You. How thankful I am that you are my ever constant. You give me the strength to stand when everything and everyone around me is changing. You are the only predictable constant in my life because You keep all Your promises that you made in your Word to me. Not one promise will You ever break, even when I break my promises to You. You are the ever-constant to me and to the whole world. As my life progresses, may I be found clinging more and more to the Rock of my salvation, my ever-present constant, my Lord and Savior, Jesus Christ!

Psalm 62:6(NLV) "He alone is my rock and my salvation, my fortress where I will not be shaken."

Journal Entry 7-22-2013

Father, I know You hear my prayers. You have answered my prayers many times although I often do not see Your answers. You have never waited for me to be perfect and get it together before You would answer. So, as I sit here, my God, in all earnestness, I am asking You to give me new spiritual eyesight. To see where the lies and demonic activity truly is, in my life, and the lives of others. I ask You to give me your supernatural strength through the Holy Spirit to rise up, cast them out, and never allow them back into my life. I want victory over it all! I'm tired of running to what will never quench my thirst. Help me to cast out this spirit of gluttony. Give me freedom and victory. Help me to have a right mindset towards food once and for all. Give me discernment and wisdom like I have never had before. I thank You for Your Word and how You have worked in my life. Raise my husband and I up to do the work and ministry You have called us to do. Help me to teach others what I learn. Create humbleness in me. Give me a new, fresh passion and touch from You. Open my eyes! Deliver me so I may be used for Your glory and honor. I am Your vessel, not Satan's vessel. These carnal desires must die!

GOD'S HEART~

WARRIOR ARISE

My Dear Child,

You asked Me to open your spiritual eyes. I am! I have been giving you glimpses of the battle you are in here on Earth for some time, now. I have been preparing you for the time that you would be ready to really see from what I have saved you, and continue to save you, from. I know that as I reveal truths to you from My Word about the evil that is all around you, it will seem overwhelming to you. Although you feel this, you must remember I am here and I am your weapon and your protection. It's time, My Child, for you to RISE UP and take your stand against all the tactics of your enemy. Take your authority that I have given you and get the enemy out of your home. Guard yourself diligently wherever you go. You are a warrior, a soldier in my army, now. I am getting you ready to put you on the front lines. I want you to lead my people to victory in their lives by teaching them what I have shown you. You are going to walk into a freedom you have never known before. It is well overdue. I have seen the torments put on you by the evil one. I have protected you in so many unseen ways in your ignorance and rebellion. I have been healing you and showering My grace all over you. I will continue to do so; but, now is the time for you to quit being on the sidelines of this battle. You must deal with things that are happening in the physical realm in a spiritual way. Everything that is happening is a result of what is unseen. Do not let anyone tell you any differently. Through prayer, My Holy Spirit, and the weapon of My Word, you have everything you need to win in the here and now! It's time to take back completely what My Son's shed blood bought for you: your freedom from the powers and principalities of this world!! So, ARISE My Warrior Child, and go in victory!!!!

Your Daddy,
God

Ephesians 6:12(NLT) "For we are not fighting against flesh-and-blood enemies, but against evil rulers and authorities of the unseen world, against mighty powers in this dark world, and against evil spirits in the heavenly places."

MY HEART~

Journal Entry 9-18-2013

The cold-hard fact is my heart is often divided. You are right in what You have been showing me. I have other lovers and I have been unwilling to let go of them. I lust and fantasize over my lover, of Food. It has the place in my heart that You should have. There have been many things that have had my heart and I am sorry, Lord. I want my heart to be fully Yours, I do. I have to say goodbye to these false lovers, these idols. Show me, Lord, how to live whole-heartedly for You. I don't want to walk in doubt, anymore. You have changed me in so many ways and, yet, I still feel so far away. I have wasted so much time pursuing my useless desires and chasing the lovers of this world. All the while, You God, my true Husband, are here waiting to love me perfectly, passionately, with abandon. I have hurt You so often only thinking of myself. Never do I give much thought in how You feel, God. As best I can, I want to change. Show me and teach me how to stay faithful to You. I am tired of these lovers sucking the life from me, never loving me in return. I know I am your child, Lord, but You have been rebuking me because You love me. It's not about salvation, now, but about purifying me. Purge my heart of the world and its false idols. You have called me to be different, to stand out, and be a light. Show me, Lord. Make my path clear and lead the way. Protect me from the snares of the enemy and help me to be totally free from this world. I love You my Lord, not like I should, but more than I used to. I thank You for the pressure of Your love not allowing me to be comfortable with my old lovers, anymore. Help me to forsake them.

THE PURGE

Oh, Lord, how I need You to help me purge the ways of this world out of me. So many things have been ingrained into me that seem right in people's eyes, but it only leads me on a path to death, (Proverbs 14:12). This is not only a physical death, but a death of emotional stability and right thinking. I need a deep, to the core of myself, inner purging of everything that I have loved in this world so that I may truly love You, the One who loved me first. I am still so polluted inside with the impurities of the sin-filled life that I lived before I came to the knowledge of Your saving grace, and let You in my heart. Each morning, as I awake, starts a new day that I must choose to purge my mind of the old way of thinking by getting in Your Word and allowing Your thoughts and truths to remove the sediment of the old me. Purge me, Holy Spirit, of all that must be gone so that I can truly live in the freedom that Jesus purchased for me. There is so much that this world seems to offer, but it is fleeting and can vanish in an instant. Stir in me a restlessness that will not stop until I am totally surrendered to allowing You to purge from me all that You want gone in my life. Purify my heart with new revelations of the God You truly are, not the God I want You to be. Purge the lies from me that I still, sometimes, believe: that I am guilty and condemned. The stigma is gone, washed away when Jesus died on the cross for me and all of mankind. I am no longer guilty because Jesus took my guilty charge and put it on Himself. Oh, Lord, purge from me and all Your people the lies we have believed. We live in a time that is becoming darker and more deceptive. Let the purging begin in Your children so that Your love will shine through us and lead Your wandering children back home to Your loving arms.

GOD'S HEART~

FALSE LOVERS

My Dear Child,

My hand is heavy upon you. This is what you are feeling. How long will you keep returning to your false lovers? Over and over, I watch you fall into their seduction. You must leave them for good. Return to Me. I am here. I have never left you; but, these lovers, these idols, in your mind separate you from the reality of My presence. You are Mine. Nothing will ever change that, but each time you give into the seduction of these lovers it makes you doubt that you belong to Me. My Child, quit doing this!! Quit allowing your heart to be divided. Recognize whose voices you are hearing when these lovers beckon you. Sometimes, it is the voice of your own flesh, because your flesh is constantly warring against My Spirit in you. Other times, it is Satan, himself, and his imps luring you away from Me. Oh, My Child, I am the true, satisfying Lover of your soul. I am a jealous God and I want to be all things to you. I will provide all that you need. I want to be the one that you run to when you are overwhelmed and fearful. You must allow Me to purge these lovers of the world from you. The more you come to Me, the more you will want Me, the true and lasting Lover of your soul. Do you want peace? Do you want joy? Then, let these lovers go! Stop answering when they are calling your name. I want to be the only Voice that you answer to. I love you, My Child!

Your Daddy,
God

James 4:4-6 (MSG) "You're cheating on God. If all you want is your own way, flirting with the world every chance you get, you end up enemies of God and his way. And do you suppose God doesn't care? The proverb has it that "he's a fiercely jealous lover." And what he gives in love is far better than anything else you'll find. It's common knowledge that "God goes against the willful proud; God gives grace to the willing humble."

MY HEART~

Journal Entry 10-8-2013

Holy Spirit, teach me and help me to hear You more clearly than I ever have. Break this will in me so that I only desire You. Consecrate me and have Your way in me. Change my perspective to Yours. I thank You for what You are doing in my heart. Show me how to be bare before You, Lord. Take all of me! Take this flesh and have Your way. I surrender as best I know how, today. I rebuke any condemnation that may come my way. You love me and I choose to believe Your Word! Freedom! I am free in You! I am not bound by the chains any longer. I can say, 'No,' and walk away from these shackles. Your Spirit lives in me, so I am free. I've been free. Now, I just have to walk in that freedom. You are the boss of my life. Forgive me for trying to run it myself. You are the Great I AM, Yahweh Jehovah, the One! Have me, Lord. Take me away in You. Manifest Your power in me and shine it forth. Take my writing and use it for Your glory. Any way You want it. I will write it and glorify Your name. You are worthy!!!

GOD'S HEART~

SPIRITUAL SURGERY

My Dear Child,

Oh, how I have wanted you to just allow Me to have My way in you. I want to pour all that I am into your very being! As you let Me move through the places that you are afraid to go, I will do surgery through My Holy Spirit. It will hurt for a time, but I promise that time will be short. Then, you will arise in a new way and become incredibly strong through My Spirit. Your desires for this world will become so faded you will wonder how you stayed in that old muck for so long. You are free, My Child, and you are going to start living out that truth. Just make Me first every day and I will do the work. You have been doing it yourself; so, that is why it seems impossible. Show Me your weakness and watch Me shine powerfully in you. I desire that! I am for you, not against you. Always remember that! I love you!

Your Daddy,
God

1 Peter 4:1-2 "So then, since Christ suffered physical pain, you must arm yourselves with the same attitude he had, and be ready to suffer, too. For if you have suffered physically for Christ, you have finished with sin.[2] You won't spend the rest of your lives chasing your own desires, but you will be anxious to do the will of God."

MY HEART~

Journal Entry 10-27-2013

To my amazing God, You are wonderfully good to me. You are so merciful and ever patient with my restless heart. You know my needs and my family's needs! Help my family and I to know the correct way. Guide us with the cars. I know I don't need a Camaro, but if You could work it all out to where we would have another vehicle, I want it! This is just a request, a want from Your daughter. You are my Daddy and I have to listen to You on this because You know what is best. Help us with the finances. Bring the abundance and overflow, the blessings, Lord, so we can fulfill Your call in the counseling ministry, and wherever You lead us.

Thank You for teaching me more and more about myself and who You have made me to be. You are working in my mind and helping me understand so much. Oh, God, please don't stop. Fill me up with Your purpose and plans. I feel so wonderful when I am doing what You have purposed for me to do. It's so wonderful and fulfilling. I am becoming more content in myself and where You have me. Things have changed a lot in my heart. I know You are still perfecting me, working in me to push me towards Your purposes and Will. Thank You, my Lord and Savior, Jesus, for all Your mercy, and forgiveness, and giving me life abundant in You. I love You so much. Have Your way in me, Your imperfect, sometimes rebellious daughter. Thank You for choosing to love me.

GOD'S HEART~

JUST ASK

My Dear Child,

You have misunderstood My heart towards you for many years. You do not have to beg and beg for Me to give you good things. I am a giver and I desire to give you an overflowing abundance of all that is good. All through My Word, I tell My people to ask. Do you know what you do when you ask? You are stepping out of independence into utter dependence upon Me. This makes Me smile! Although you don't feel like you trust Me sometimes, or believe that I will answer you, the very fact that you are requesting of Me to do something shows that you know you need Me. Each time you make your requests known to Me, you are chipping away a little more of your self reliance. Asking requires you to lay down your pride. Pride is rooted in self reliance. My Child, you cannot rely on even yourself for very long. Others let you down and are often unreliable, but eventually you will even let yourself down. You are not reliable to give even yourself what you need. I am the only one who you were made to rely on. I made you! Every intricate detail of who you are was designed by Me. I know what you truly need and, even, what you don't need. I desire to protect you, guide you, and, most of all, bless you with so much goodness that it overflows to everyone you come in contact with. So, My Child, keep asking! It's ok to do that. I'm just waiting to answer you!

Your Daddy,
God

Matthew 7:7(ESV) "Ask, and it will be given to you; seek, and you will find; knock, and it will be opened to you."

MY HEART~

Journal Entry 12-11-2013

Thank You so much, Lord, for giving me the Camaro. Never did I think You would move on my husband's heart like You did to surprise me with such a wonderful blessing. It is a gift from You first because all good things come from above. Then it is from my awesome man, whom You have given me. Oh, Father, how You have worked in my life. You use me and bless me, despite my sin and weakness. Your grace is amazing. I love you, Lord. Use me more and more. Give me a boldness and confidence like I have never had. Help me to remember that I am the sweet aroma of You wherever I go.

Journal Entry 12-22-2013

I don't know what You are trying to teach me, Lord, but help me to get it. Show me where I am wrong and where I am right. You gave me this strong will, help me to balance it. Please, help me not to doubt what you have shown me and spoken to me. Why do certain things disturb me so much? Is it a stirring from You or is it just my flesh? Are you trying to prepare me for the persecution that will become even more intense as I serve and follow You? Help me to not care so much about the opinions of others. Help me to forgive myself when I fail. I'm tired of doubting Your acceptance and love. Just when I think I'm secure and get more confident in You, something happens and all the fear and self-doubt come swooping in. Show me where I am wrong and help me to not feel condemnation. Thank You for Your constant mercy. I need it so much!

GOD'S HEART~

BLESSED TO BE A BLESSING

My Dear Child,

I told you a few weeks ago to just ask! Ask Me for whatever it is on your heart. I don't care if it's a request for a material possession, or a need for someone else, or something you want Me to help you change about yourself. When you are talking to Me, and asking, it deepens our relationship. Too often, you keep your distance from Me thinking I am mad at you and don't want to truly help you. My heart is always full of pure love for you. I am full of goodness. There is no evil in Me.

I gave you the Camaro as a gift, one that you requested. Do you remember asking Me? You knew you did not need it, but you thought it was beautiful and would be something fun to have. You put it to the back of your mind because you knew it was a want, not a need. I saw that My Child. I moved on the heart of your husband so I could surprise you and give you not only your needs, but your wants as well. I knew you were ready for it, and I want to show my heart towards you. You are my delightful daughter whom I see as very beautiful and wonderfully created. I desire to bestow good gifts to you. Each time you look at this beautiful car, I want you to remember that I desire to give all abundance to you in this life. This abundance is not only in the spiritual, but also in the material. I love you, and if I would give up My Only Son, Jesus, to die on a cross for you, then why would I not freely give you all other things? Think about that! You have seen how some of my other children judge their brother's and sister's motives when I have chosen to bless them. They are tearing down and judging. This breaks My heart. This has disturbed you, and you are correct in this feeling for it is My Holy Spirit who lives inside of you who is grieved by this. I want to prepare you, and help you learn how to stand unmoved when unfair, and untrue judgment comes against you. It will happen, My Child! You have seen how it has wavered you when you have made a stand, and spoke out against this, and you were persecuted for it. You are learning, as I teach you through My Spirit, to not doubt what I have spoken and shown to you. My desire is to train you and all My children to always edify and lift up, not tear down. I am the one who judges the heart and I want all My children to leave that job to Me. Let My Spirit lead you, not the opinion of how others perceive things. I desire to bless, bless, bless, so you can be a blessing to others!

Your Daddy,
God

Matthew 7:11(NLT) "So if you sinful people know how to give good gifts to your children, how much more will your heavenly Father give good gifts to those who ask Him?"

MY HEART~

Journal Entry 2-6-2014

What is wrong with me? Why can I not just obey You? What is it? Where am I at really? I feel horrible! I want to feel love. I want to know Your love, but there is a block. Is it my lack of faith and trust? Do I really have any at all? Open my eyes. Help me to see where I am blind. Help me to see where I am deceiving myself. Thank You for loving and being patient with me.

SPIRITUAL AMNESIA

Wake me up from my spiritual amnesia. Like a heavy fog that rolls in upon the land and makes it difficult to see, this is what it feels like when the amnesia comes in on the landscape of my mind. I forget who I am in Christ. I no longer remember that the only thing that makes me right before God is faith in Jesus. When this amnesia comes, I go back to the insanity of my futile thinking. Through this thinking, in my amnesia, selfishness comes out like a roaring lion. The doors to self-pity, self-indulgence, and self-reliance are opened, once again. I can't see past myself, how I'm feeling, and all that is wrong with me. Darkness engulfs me and depression sets in on me. I want to scream, 'Get me out of my head!' Then, I hear a Voice. A Voice that is different from my own. It is tender, sweet, and ever-so-loving in tone. Then, it happens! My memory is triggered once again by the Holy Spirit who lives in me. He brings me out of my amnesia. The fog has lifted and I can clearly see, once again. I can see myself through the eyes of Christ, and the ones around me this way, too. He brings sanity back to my thinking and I have a sound mind with sound judgment, once again.

 Oh, how thankful I am that no matter how often this amnesia overtakes me, the Holy Spirit has not forgotten who I am. He reminds me often that my righteousness is permanent because of Christ. He, also, reminds me that I can learn to recognize when the amnesia is coming and fight it while I can still see through the fog by running to His Word.

I praise Jesus that He has won the victory over my spiritual amnesia! In His love for me, He will not let me forget for too long. He will always do whatever it takes to trigger my memory of all that He has done for me. I am all of a sudden reminded that my Jesus, also, has amnesia. He has chosen to have amnesia towards my sin, for He say's in His Word that, "my sins He will remember no more." He has cast them as far as the east is to the west. What an amazing Savior He is!

Hebrews 10:17(NLT) "Then he says, "I will never again remember their sins and lawless deeds."

GOD'S HEART~

YOU ARE RETRIEVED

My Dear Child,

You are Mine! You just read in John that you were Mine before I sent My Son, Jesus, to the Earth. I know that is hard to wrap your head around, but all you need to understand is that Jesus bought you back from sin and death. I sent Jesus into the world to retrieve all those who would believe in Him. Although it is not My desire for any to perish, not all will receive My Son. I want you to be established in the truth that you have received My Son. You are getting better and better at truly trusting Me, but there is still healing to be done. I want you to listen, really listen, to Me. Yes, write what I say. You have had it confirmed, now do it. This will clarify My Voice to you. Your mind is running away from My Spirit, and you are trying to fix and find solutions to all that plagues you. Yes, I have given you a strong will, so you naturally think you have to fix and control all that life brings you. Oh, My Sweet, Little One, you cannot! I am already in your future, so do I not know how to help you? You have to give up control to Me. That requires a deeper trust in Me. You don't have to be afraid to let Me in all the dark places. I will shine My light in and make sense of things. I will make you whole. Just let Me. Be with Me! I love you, I love you, I love you!!! Get that established so deep in your heart that nothing will shake you. I am establishing you in so many ways. Just be patient with Me and with yourself. Keep seeking Me as I lead you. I love you.

Your Daddy,
God

Colossians 2:7(NLT) "Let your roots grow down into him, and let your lives be built on him. Then your faith will grow strong in the truth you were taught, and you will overflow with thankfulness."

MY HEART~

Journal Entry 3-26-2014

It's so hard to let go of control and give it all to You. Just when I think I'm letting go, my strong will creeps right back in. There are so many places in my heart I try to hide from You. So many coping mechanisms I have, developed over the years. When fear creeps in, I go into 'Connie's- got- this' mode. I can fix this. I'll just do this myself. I can't, Dear Jesus. I can't fix anything or provide what I need. Why do I try? I am so weak in my own strength. I can't control or make anyone do anything, so why do I try? Why do I get this way with people? I want friendships so badly within our church. Since being in this church, there have been many people I have come to love, and after emotionally investing myself, they leave. I hate it! I miss my family and friends in Illinois so badly and, yet, I know you want us here. Help me to be at peace with that.

THE QUICKSAND

I hate this flesh! I get so tired of the carnality that comes up in me. Some days, I get so lost in it. It's like quicksand. The moment I start letting my fleshly thoughts, and actions, lead the way is the moment I start to sink. The more I try to get myself out, the deeper I go into that sinking sand. I need to stop at the moment that I step into the quicksand. I need to cry out to my Daddy God to lift me out. In one mighty swoop, He will put me back on the solid, firm path. Most often, I fight God by trying to figure my own way out, leaving me utterly exhausted and weak. I know that He often gives me warning signs that the path I am about to go on is dangerous, but He allows me the choice of which way to go. He knows that the more I try to keep control, and figure everything out, the weaker I will become. That is right where He wants me. Because in that weakness, I will cry out, and that is when He can come and be that strength for me. I know, this is called surrender. He just wants me to surrender my will to His everyday. In that surrender, I will avoid the quicksand and thorny patches that often leave me bruised and torn up.

I wonder if it will ever be easy to surrender. Surrendering requires for me to ignore and kill that fleshly voice that is always screaming at me. When has dying ever been easy? I know it wasn't easy for my Savior Jesus. He left His perfect, heavenly home, to come to this sin filled world, and become flesh like me. He heard the voice of His flesh tempting Him to give in, but He chose obedience to His Father. I am so glad He did. Even though I sometimes walk right into the quicksand in this earthly life, He has saved me from the eternal quicksand of Hell. Thank you, Jesus!

Hebrews 4: 15, 16(NLT) "This High Priest of ours understands our weakness, for he faced all of the same testing we do, yet he did not sin. So, let us come boldly to the throne of our gracious God. There we will receive his mercy, and we will find grace to help us when we need it most."

GOD'S HEART~

EVERY NOOK AND CRANNY

My Dear Child,

Do you know how much I want you to know Me? I want you to know Me in such a way that all your fears are released. I want to free you of all that holds you back. You must allow Me to enter into all the nooks and crannies of your soul.

Your nooks are the places that you have secluded and isolated yourself from Me. It's the parts of you that you don't want anyone to know or see. Those are the parts where you think I am disappointed in you. To truly know who I am, you must come out of that corner, your nook. You see in that nook is not only isolation from your Healer, but there are many crannies everywhere. These are the places in your soul that have been cracked and opened up by your sin and the sin of others. Some of these crannies are just a very small opening. You don't even know they are there. Others are deep and long. They have produced a great deal of infection in your soul. This oozes out in your behavior. These are your coping mechanisms. You must allow My Spirit into those areas. I will be your new coping mechanism.

Come to the secret place with Me everyday and watch Me heal you wholly and completely. I am your antibiotic for these infections. You have been learning and growing so much by My Spirit these past few years. You have come a long way, but we have so much more to share together. The secret place has been a missing element in our relationship; you are beginning to see how critically important it is. I could allow you to stay where you are at with Me, but I want a close, uninhibited relationship with you! If you allow yourself to come to the secret place, you will hear Me more clearly, and become more intimate with Me.

My Child, let's go the nooks and crannies of your soul together.

I will convince you so completely of just how much I love you that you will never want to hide in your nook, again. I will be your new hiding place.

Your Daddy,
God

Psalms 32:7(NASB) "You are my hiding place; You preserve me from trouble; You surround me with songs of Deliverance."

MY HEART~

Journal Entry 4-16-2014

Father, here I am coming to You. I need You to settle my mind and my spirit. I want to trust that You have it all under control. There are so many changes coming with moving out of the parsonage and away from the church. It all seems overwhelming and financially impossible, but You say with You it is all possible. Help this weak child.

GOD'S HEART~

GRANTED STRENGTH

My Dear Child,

You just read in Timothy how I have granted you the strength and made you able to do the ministry that I have called you to do. I have appointed you; therefore, I will lead you and take care of you. I know your mind is racing once again. You have done the right thing by coming to Me and letting it all out. Pour out your concerns on Me and let them go. Remember, I told you they are too heavy to carry? I know your need. I know you have a hard time resting in My care, but I will show you, time and time again, that all your needs will be met. Concentrate on today with Me. Commit to coming to the secret place with Me everyday. No matter how awkward it feels and unsure that you are, just come! Will you do that? If you do, I will do amazing things in you, and we will become closer. Your self-interest and your fears will subside.

Don't worry about your daughter. I will take care of her and work in her. You don't have to figure her life out. You are not responsible for her, I am. I will use you to help her, but I will direct you in how to do that.

Don't fret about money. It's all provided for. I have more than enough provision for you. It's on its way, I promise. Just keep going forward and keep reaching out with My love. Not your own love because it will fail. Let peace reside deep in your heart. I see, I know, I will provide. I love you.

Your Daddy,
God

Isaiah 40:28-29(NASB) "Do you not know? Have you not heard? The Everlasting God, the LORD, the Creator of the ends of the earth Does not become weary or tired. His understanding is inscrutable. He gives strength to the weary, and to him who lacks might He increases power."

MY HEART~

Journal Entry 4-17-2014

I praise you, my Lord! You are amazing. The work Your Spirit has done in me is truly a miracle. You have given me greater purpose and passion. You have loved me so patiently, thank You! I love You. Give me more of You. Show me more of who You truly are. Give me Your power and confidence in that power. I want worry and anxiety to disappear. Help me to overcome this flesh every day. Give me clear direction and open the doors for my writing and books. I am holding You to that Word You gave me that there would be books. Show me how You want it done. Use them to speak to Your people and to the lost. I will go where You send me. I know I may throw a fit from time to time but I believe that will happen less and less. You are speaking to me through these writings. My own hand that has written them has been Your Spirit directing me. Help me to stay encouraged in that. Fight discouragement for me. I love You Father. Thank You for all You have done for me and what You will do in the future.

GOD'S HEART~

GET READY

My Dear Child,

Oh, how my Spirit is stirring you up inside. I am getting you ready to step into a much bigger realm of influence for Me; as well as a deeper understanding of My amazing love for you!! What I have been preparing and training you to do is about to be fully birthed in your life. As this new transition is happening, you will become easily overwhelmed and frustrated if you do not continually abide in My Presence. You must remember that I already have your course laid out for you. I will provide at just the right timing everything you need. Don't waste your time trying to figure out the how's and when's. Just rest and trust when I say, it will be soon. Leave all the details to Me. I want you to focus on what I tell you to do for today. You may keep that exciting expectation of what the future holds in the forefront of your mind. This will help you to keep moving forward. But, remember it is not your job to get things done and make them happen. I know exactly how to delegate what needs to be done. I will speak to the hearts of My children whom I want to use to help you. I want you to enjoy this journey that I am taking you on. You cannot do that if you are trying to figure everything out. Rest in My Lordship and, remember, I am already in your future. I see and know all. Learn to relax in My Sovereignty. Just walk with Me, one step at a time, and be in the 'here and now' of your life. You can be assured that before you know it, the greatness of the future that I have for you will soon be a very real 'here and now' reality. Get excited, anticipate, and cherish every moment of your life as I take you into your future that I have planned for you. I love you more than you can fathom.

Your Daddy,
God

2 Corinthians 9:8 (ESV) "And God is able to make all grace abound to you, so that having all sufficiency in all things at all times, you may abound in every good work."

GOD'S HEART`

JUST SHOW UP

My Dear Child,

I know you are tired this morning, but you did it. You got up and showed up to meet with Me. Be patient and do not try to anticipate what I want to do while we are in the secret place. Just, meet Me there.

Many years ago, the seed of My Kingdom was planted into you. You did not realize how My Word was working in you. Although you were young in your understanding, your desire to seek My Word was there. You put the Word in you. You listened and you meditated more than you give yourself credit for. Do you not see how I have been adding more and more to your life? You have more of My wisdom. You are showing more love and compassion, and you have more territory. You see My Child, the years before I gave you your husband, Willie, and sent you to Texas, there was much happening in you. The seed of My Word was planted in you and the harvest of that is what is happening, now. My Kingdom has grown up in you. You have new understanding. I am, now, making you someone whom others can run to for comfort, shelter, and safety. You will be a great teacher of My Word and you will be My seed planter. You will help others see My Kingdom. For some, you will be the harvester. Just continue in My Word and I will guide you to know what each person needs. You will be My nourisher of the seeds that have been planted in others.

I am promoting you once again, so take great care to what I have entrusted to you. You are going to see many blessings overflow to you. Always remember Whose hand they come from. I love you.

Your Daddy,
God

John 4:37-38(NASB) "For in this case the saying is true, 'One sows and another reaps. I sent you to reap that for which you have not labored; others have labored and you have entered into their labor."

MY HEART~

Journal Entry 5-20-2014

I need You to settle my mind. I miss You, Lord. So much change coming with moving and so much to do. I need You, I know, and yet I don't make the time for You like I should. It's so easy to get distracted in this world. It seems when family is visiting, I am zapped. I know it is on me to make You a priority.

THE DISTRACTIONS

Distractions, they are everywhere! I find that some days I am in a constant state of distraction. There is interference everywhere I turn. The dark forces of this world will do whatever it takes to draw my attention away from God. The moment I am diverted, I am no longer abiding through my mind, in His Presence and then, I forget truth. I forget my identity and position in Christ.

Distractions produce a mental state characterized by a lack of clear and orderly thought and behavior. This is just plain and simply stated as confusion. I have the power of the living God in me. When I walk in the authority that Jesus has given me, nothing is impossible for me. I can heal, cast out demons, and tread on all evil that comes before me. I can say to my mountain move and it will move. All this is possible as I abide and remember who I am.

It makes sense to me, now, why I must give careful thought as to how I spend my day. The seemingly harmless activities of my former life now take on a whole new meaning. I cannot afford to be distracted with the things of my former life. There are places where I used to go and things that I used to do that I just can't to do anymore. I have been chosen to step out of the former way of doing things into a new life and a new way of thinking. I am set apart, no longer a citizen of this world, but

I am a heavenly citizen. I am a now a foreigner in this land and my home is not here.

When I give my attention to the distractions of this temporary place my mind becomes muddied. I am unable to give my full attention to the Lord and what He is speaking to me. The distractions of this world are an obstacle to my concentration of the things that really matter. Even in watching or listening to something that seems to be harmless, I can become distracted and drawn away from truth. Everything I put in front of my eyes and into my ear's affects me in some way. I must always be mindful of this and on guard because, I have an enemy who is intent on distracting me from the true desires the Lord has put in my heart. Within those desires, is my purpose the Lord has given me to fulfill while I am here in this world.

GOD'S HEART~

MISSING YOU

My Dear Child,

It's been a long time since you have come to Me. I'm right here sustaining every move you make. I know you miss Me and I miss you when life takes you away from Me. You will just have to decide to make time for me everyday. Yes, it seems life is getting busier, and there is change coming, but you can prioritize. You must take control of your time or it will control you. You do not have too much put on you. You can do everything that I tell you to do. It's when you do things that I have not ordered you to do that you get overwhelmed.

Listen closely for My voice. I will prioritize for you. Focus on your life right here. That's all you have to do. I love you so much. Remember to take time to write. It is a gift from Me to you and I want you to give it to others. I will lead you in what to write and how to write. Only look to Me. I am using your writing to touch lives and for others to see My glory. Let this passion, which is My passion in you, drive you forward. There will be books. I have spoken it to you, My promise to you. Just trust Me to make it happen. Just wait and see how much more I have for you to write. It will flow out of you. Remember, enjoy the journey of change. I love you!

Your Daddy,
God

Psalm 90:12 (NIV) "Teach us to number our days, that we may gain a heart of wisdom."

MY HEART~

CHANGES

We spend our days fighting change. God says, 'Enjoy the journey of change. Do not fear it but welcome it.'

In our humanness, we need change. We so easily attach ourselves to people, places, and things that are not good for us. If things did not change, we would never move forward. God uses change to grow us up. He uses change to help us see our need for Him. When sudden change comes it shakes us out of our complacency. It moves us from a place of independence to a place of utter dependence upon the One who created us. It is our fleshly, sin nature to live life independent and apart from God. This way of living must be broken in our lives. We must change our way of thinking. We must change our way of living. God always desires to change us for the better. This is called transformation. Change helps us to transform into who God wants us to be. Change pushes us forward when we have our heels stuck in the ground, refusing to move, and do something different. God uses change to purify, refine, and break rebellion in us. All of our life, things are changing. Our bodies change, seasons change, circumstances change, culture changes, feelings change, and on it goes. We cannot escape it. If God did not allow change, how would we ever learn to know and appreciate the One who never changes, the Lord God Almighty? He is our Rock. He is steady, consistent, and stable. He does not change His mind about loving us. His goodness and mercy are unchanging throughout our entire life. As we keep our mind and heart towards Him, we can learn to embrace all the changes that will inevitably come our way.

Hebrews 13:8 (NIV) "Jesus Christ is the same yesterday, today and forever."

ENDURE THE PRESSURE

I can feel the pressure building. It is a force that compels me to act. It is that old nature of sin working within my soul. The moment I feel this pressure coming on, feels like a matter of urgency that demands my attention. Most often, I have a legitimate desire that needs fulfillment. My enemy, Satan, or my own evil desires lurking within tells me to get it met apart from God and His direction. This is the moment of choice! I can choose to endure through the pressure and surrender to God. I can allow Him to do His perfecting work in me, or I can submit to my flesh. I have a choice to believe the lies that make me cave in under the pressure or, cast the lies out of my mind. I have always disliked pressure and have been quick to relieve it any way that I can. I am learning that without pressure, I will continue in the same oppressive condition. Sometimes, the pressure is directly from the hand of God, imploring me to do things differently. It is of great necessity to get all rebellion out of my life. God uses this pressure to lovingly move me to choose the truth instead of lies. How easily I forget who I am in Christ. I have the power, dominion, and the ability to subdue this flesh and its evil cravings. I don't have to accept every thought that comes as truth. I don't have to act on every temptation. I don't have to say everything that comes into my head, out of my mouth. When I speak something, I give it power, whether good or bad. When I am feeling pressure, I can see it as a warning sign that something isn't right in my thinking and doing. I can welcome the pressure and submit it to Christ's authority living in me. There is often pain in pressure. If I let God have His way in me through the pressure, His righteousness will come forth in my actions. He will, then, be manifested through me to a world that so desperately needs to see Him. So, I choose this day to allow the pressure to produce all that God desires for me. I will stand firm in my position through the pressure! All glory going to God who sustains me!

Journal Entry 6-14-2014

Take me out of this place, Lord. I am angry and battling myself. Why don't You help me? Where are You? What are You doing? I'm tired, Lord, so very tired of the battle. I see You touch others, and give them power, even while they are in their sin. Why can't You change me? What am I doing thinking You want to use me? I'm a mess. A mess that often pretends to have it together. I don't. I am a complete disaster if You do not step in and do whatever it is that I cannot do on my own. Ok, I have rebellion. Don't we all? How do I stop it? It hurts and the pressure is growing in me. I feel like I'm going to burst if You don't do something. I need You to revive me, Holy Spirit. Give me Your power. When will You do it for me? When? I'm angry. Everything is changing. I hate it. I hate it and I don't know the way to go, anymore. So, there it is. Do You still love me? If it's not about what I do, but what You have done, then why do I battle security in You? Get rid of these demons for me. Release them off of me, please!!!

GOD'S HEART~

THE PLAN

My Dear Child,

The roots of rejection are deep within you, My Child. In your mother's womb, you felt it because the great deceiver of your soul was there. He had a plan, but My great love for you cancelled out all his plans. He thought he would surely destroy you by using your adoption to produce feelings of being cast out and abandoned. Oh, but My dear, precious Child, **abandoned you were not, for I knew exactly where you were**. He thought he was ordering your destruction, but I was setting you up for your greatness.

On he goes sending his imps to do his destructive deeds in your life. Your enemy says, 'I will send more rejection and abandonment from the ones who are supposed to love her. Then, she will be open to receive the spirit of fear that I will send her. This way she will always have doubt and be untrusting of everyone you send, especially Jesus.'

I, the Lord God declares, 'She is mine. I call it out, so it will be!'

So, the deceiver goes on with his plan. Your enemy says, 'I will send a spirit of bondage to her so she will never be free. She will become so enslaved to worldly pleasures. She will never see how much Jesus loves her. Then, she will be ready for my perverse spirit to come in. This spirit will bring her so much confusion about what love is, she will do almost anything with anyone. After all, my imps of perversity have a right to be there from the sins of her ancestors. Her ancestors did not know their spiritual authority through Jesus, and she never will either. I will pass them to her children for further destruction. Oh, my plan is great!'

I, the Lord God declares, '**The curse has been broken through My Son, Jesus, shed blood.** She **WILL** know this and take her authority one day. You are already under her feet. My mighty Holy Spirit will lead her into **ALL** truth. For all the people you sent that you used to crush her, I will send double that to build her back up. I will use them to show her that I am real and who I really am. I will build her up in my love.'

Your enemy says, 'I just can't have that. I will send the spirit of heaviness to invade her. She will be in such darkness and depression with a broken heart that she will never find her way out. She may have received your Son, Jesus, but I will constantly be there to feed her doubt. She will be in despair. There will be no way out!'

I, the Lord her God declares, **'I am the light in the darkness. I will pull her out Myself with My transforming power. She is Mine!** While you thought you were destroying her, I was purifying her. When you thought she was at her breaking point, I was producing a steadfast warrior. She will be a warrior that will know and recognize when you are active in other's lives. She will be My hands and feet of love to them. She will proclaim the truth to a world that is in darkness.'

My Child, do you see the plan of your enemy? Do you see My plan? It is coming forth. Now, go and proclaim freedom to the captives as you walk into your total freedom. The deceiver's plans have been cancelled. They are NULL and VOID! **Go forth, My anointed one!!**

Your Daddy,
God

Isaiah 61:1 "The Spirit of the Lord is upon me, because the Lord has anointed me to bring good news to the afflicted. He has sent me to bind up the brokenhearted, to proclaim liberty to the captives and freedom to the prisoners."

GOD'S HEART~

HOW LONG

My Dear Child,

I am waiting! How long will it take for you to surrender to My control? I know you are miserable. You must stop running from Me. Can't you see I am your only true comfort in this world? How many times do you have to go back to your worldly comforts? It is YOU I am waiting for. You must choose to surrender your rebellion which is rooted in your distrust of Me. It won't be easy, but if you want the good emotions to come, and to stay, then you must stay surrendered. Trust Me to give you your needs. I know what you need. Where is your faith in Me? I can only be as big as you allow Me to be in your life. Quit making Me little so I can give you a big future. I WANT TO! I love you!

Your Daddy,
God

Jeremiah 32:27 (NIV) "I am the Lord, the God of all mankind. Is anything too hard for me?"

MY HEART~

Journal Entry 6-30-2014

Oh, my Jesus, You have been waiting on me to just believe who I really am. You want me to walk in a realm of possibilities with You! When the mountains come at me, remind me that it is not a mountain. It's just how I am seeing it, my perception of a false reality. Reality is what I cannot see through my carnal eyes. The enemy really does have many tricked. I'm sorry, Lord, for my own self-reliance. I want to be led by Your Spirit! This flesh lies to me and I'm tired of it. I must deprive it. Remind me of that every moment. I love You Jesus, You are so amazing!

GOD'S HEART~

NOT THE SAME

My Dear Child,

You are not the same! There was an impartation to you last night of a magnitude that you cannot fully comprehend at this time. Day-by-day, you will experience this as it comes out of you by My Spirit. I have set you forth with new power. Believe it, speak it, and walk it out. I told you My plans are big for you, that I was waiting on you. Now, speak and declare that you believe and it will be. The fruit of your lips, what you speak, and believe is what you will produce. I have been waiting for you to forsake the lies and believe what I have said. As you have been teaching others, I have been teaching you. The truth I have shown you by My Word is setting you free and that is what will keep you free. You have new power over the enemy now, because you were imparted new truth last night. Keep yourself aware of My presence and you will not forget your identity. Above everything else, you must make time for Me. As you spend time with Me, you will mirror Me naturally. Give your attention to Heavenly pursuits. Remember, you are two dimensional. Let who you already are in the heavenlies, reflect into the world. You are in Christ and Christ is in you. Keep your rightful position. No longer allow identity theft from the evil one. I love you.

Your Daddy,
God

Ephesians 2:6 (NLT) "For he raised us from the dead along with Christ and seated us with him in the heavenly realms because we are united with Christ Jesus."

GOD'S HEART~

8-1-2014 A Word Spoken to You by Your Husband from God:

Songs 2:10-14 (HCSB)
[10] "My love calls to me: Arise, my darling. Come away, my beautiful one."
[11] "For now the winter is past; the rain has ended and gone away."
[12] "The blossoms appear in the countryside. The time of singing has come, and the turtledove's cooing is heard in our land."
[13] "The fig tree ripens its figs; the blossoming vines give off their fragrance. Arise, my darling. Come away, my beautiful one."
[14] "My dove, in the clefts of the rock, in the crevices of the cliff, let me see your face, let me hear your voice; for your voice is sweet, and your face is lovely."

When I read this, this morning, I thought of you, My Sweetheart. You truly are like the spring flowers. Over the past four years, I have seen you blossom into a beautiful flower. From the day I met you, I thought you were the most beautiful woman I had ever met. I have seen something happen over the past four years in you, a transformation. Not like a simple change of hair or a change of how you dress, but much deeper than that. Your transformation has been from the inside out. With that transformation, I have seen a glow appear in you, and a certain thing that I could not ever put the right words to describe. But this Song of Songs describes it best when it says, 'winter is gone and spring has come.' I see your winter has gone and your spring has come forth. Along with the spring, a beautiful garden full of flowers and lush vegetation has sprouted out of you. The one thing that excites me is spring is just the beginning of the new life. For as spring passes, more fruit develops, and vegetation becomes more and more flourishing. Connie, your spring has come! You are more than a beautiful flower. You are a lush garden ready to produce fruit beyond your imagination! God has purposed you for this time. Arise, My Darling!

I love you, Babe!

MY HEART~

Journal Entry 8-2-2014

I thank You, Jesus, so much for loving me through my husband. How You spoke to me yesterday through the writing You gave him. I so needed it. Song of Solomon 2:10-14, I will never for forget it. The part that sticks out to me is the dove that hides in the cleft of the rock. It's like You are telling me that You want me to talk to You. You want to hear my voice and see my beautiful face. This is something I do not do enough and its time for me to come out of hiding. Hiding is what I do so well, don't I? Forgive me, Father. I want You, I do. I need You so desperately.

GOD'S HEART~

YOUR SPRING HAS COME

My Dearest Daughter,

I love you! I want to pierce your heart so deeply with My love that you will never forget it. Yes, you are My dove, pure and blameless before Me. Come out of hiding completely, and let Me see that beautiful creation that I have been making in you. I have allowed your husband to see you through My eyes so you can see yourself that way. When he speaks a word to you from Me, listen closely and intently. You will hear Me. I have been radically transforming you these past few years. Your spring has come! If you will yield to Me, the fruit that you will begin to bear will amaze you. All who look at you will see it and see Me. They already do. But there is so much more. The enemy is defeated in your life if you will just believe that and walk in your authority. I have every answer you need, for every moment, if you will just tune into Me. Quit thinking on the things of this world. Leave it behind and find no satisfaction in it. Quit worrying about the scale and just listen for My voice to guide you. Let it go! Stop, quit, forsake it all, and cling to Me. I'm here, right here to give you what you need. I know it is not easy. I know how you feel, but you are an overcomer through My Spirit. You already have the victory, just claim the victory and don't let it go. Your winter is gone, My Dear One. Will you believe it?

Your Daddy,
God

Deuteronomy 28:7 (ESV) "The Lord will cause your enemies who rise against you to be defeated before you. They shall come out against you one way and flee before you seven ways."

MY HEART~

Journal Entry 8-18-2014

I thank you, Lord, for meeting me where I am, and for birthing in me Your purpose. I thank You for always reassuring me when I am drowning in doubt. By Your Spirit, I know Your truth. The spirit of fear has been attacking me. I must rebuke and fight back in authority. I must push through the tormenting lies. You are truly teaching me how to hear You and know what is of You. I thank You for the gift of writing You have given me. I cherish it and desire to glorify You in it. Help me to get this book done so others may know Your true heart for them. Give me an unmoving boldness, to know that I know what mission You have given me. I love You so!!

GOD'S HEART~

FULLY BELIEVE

My Dear Child,

All that needs to happen now is for you to fully believe what I have spoken to you. Then, all that is in you by My Spirit will manifest out of you and in your life. It's time for you to give birth to what I have been creating in you. You have a message from Me to give to the world around you. Don't look at what you see or listen to the whispers of doubt that come into your thoughts. Look unto Me and hear through My Spirit living inside of you. You know the truth from My Living Word. It's alive in you, growing, just waiting for you to move in faith. The spirit of fear has had its grip on you. This is not from Me. You have felt its presence, especially at night. You must fight in my authority and cast it out. You have been given a spirit of peace, love, and a sound mind. As you take your authority over this fear, your faith will have room to move. This spirit has lied to you and made you afraid of Me; although, I am the One who is totally on your side. So, I ask you again, My Sweet Child. Do you believe your winter is gone? Do not let your emotions dictate what you believe. Let My truth be your dictator. I love you, My Chosen One. **YOUR WINTER IS OVER!!!!!**

Your Daddy,
God

Isaiah 43:18-19 (ETRV) "So don't remember what happened in earlier times. Don't think about what happened a long time ago, because I am doing something new! Now you will grow like a new plant. Surely you know this is true. I will even make a road in the desert, and rivers will flow through that dry land."

A Note to the Reader

I want to thank all who have read this book and taken this journey with me. I did not know until a few months before putting this book together that God would want me to include personal journal entries. I encountered many emotions while I was going through my old journals. As I began putting the book together, I would have moments of fear with the thought of all the people who would have a glimpse into my life and know what only God knows about me. I was about to open up my life and be completely vulnerable. It would be a risk that I was taking, but that is part of walking in faith. God was telling me to keep my eyes on Him, and get out of the boat like He did Peter. So, I take the risk for the sake of the message Jesus wants to get out to YOU, the reader, He so dearly loves.

The message He has for you through sharing this personal journey is one of unconditional love, security, and acceptance. You are free to pour out everything you feel, good or bad before Him. He desires desperately to be a Daddy to you. He is not waiting for you to get rid of your sin before you come to Him. He bids you to come as you are. Receive freely his mercy, love, and grace. His invasive love for you will change and transform you.

I believe there are many like me who have battled with security in God's love for them. But they live in a silent torment. Their rebellion is deeply rooted in distrust. God wants you to know you are SECURE. He is not going anywhere. You can trust Him. He will never change His mind about you. He loves you because He wants to. All He wants you to do is BELIEVE IT!!!

I am so thankful that although I have often left God in my wanderings, and been unfaithful, He has never left me. His amazing, radical love has protected me, saved me, covered me, transformed me, and will continue to do so until He takes me home. His love will do the same for you.

BROKEN PIECES

When you take the pieces of your broken life before God, He is able to put the shattered pieces back together, again. He fixes the cracks no one can see deep in your soul. He will hold you together with the superglue of His Love. Nothing can undue this bond once you give Him permission to do the fixing. He is careful and precise at how He puts each piece of your broken life back together. It may seem at times that He is being slow in this process of putting your life back together; but, if you have put a puzzle together you know, it takes time and patience. A piece may look right, but if just one corner is wrong, it doesn't work. He has a purpose for every little piece of your life. He will use your life mightily to help mend other's brokenness; and, for you to see His ways are wonderful. Once He has put the pieces of your life back together again, it will be better than you could ever have thought of doing for yourself. When all the ugly cracks and shattered pieces of your life are put together by Him, the Master Puzzle Solver, your life will become a beautiful portrait.

Will you give Him your broken pieces?

Romans 10:9(NLT)

"If you confess with your mouth that Jesus is Lord and believe in your heart that God raised him from the dead, you will be saved!"

If you would like to order more copies of this book you can go to Connie's website at www.conniemiller.online or at www.amazon.com. You may also contact Connie personally by email at gods.girl41@hotmail.com. You may also request a special-order copy at your local Lifeway Christian Book Store.

Made in the USA
Lexington, KY
10 December 2019